I0483429

Nobis

MAKING OTHERS SEE

Pensacola Chapter
National League of American Pen Women

Nobis, Copyright ©2016 by Pensacola Chapter National League of American Pen Women. All rights reserved. Printed in the United States of America; no part of this book may be used or reproduced in any manner whatsoever without written permission, except in the case of brief quotations embodied in critical articles and reviews.

First Edition published 2016

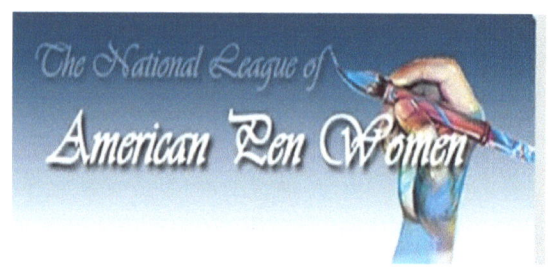

Cover art "Dancers" by Mara Viksnins
Karen McAferty Morris, Editor
Cover design by Mac McGovern

Copyright © 2016 Pensacola Chapter NLAPW
All rights reserved.

All rights remain with the respective artists included in this work.

ISBN-13:978-0692566312
ISBN-10:0692566317

Making Others See

Cast your mind back to the days of the Impressionists. Edgar Degas, a notable artist from that era, mastered depicting movement as seen in the renditions of his famous dancers. Like Degas' dancers, the members of the National League of American Pen Women, Pensacola Branch #84 are dancers together. We learn from each other and enjoy fellowship. We have sorted through our ideas and are ready to accept and conquer new vistas. This book highlights our journey. It is both introspective and reflective, yet also enlightening. This book was put together with great care to show how women artists, poets, writers, photographers, and crafters with divergent backgrounds, unique skills, and personal ideals could come together in harmony.

"Nobis," the name we chose for our endeavor, is the Latin word for "Us." The esprit de corps among our members has resulted in the creation of this book. In a world of disconnects, impersonal relationships, and confusing realities, it is a comfort to find a place to take delight in, and enjoy art and poetry. Degas said, **"Art is not what you see, but what you make others see."** We hope this book takes you to a special place. We hope you will appreciate our efforts to make others see.

Mara Viksnins, President

"Every day we should hear at least one little song, read one good poem, see one exquisite picture, and, if possible, speak a few sensible words."

Johann Wolfgang von Goethe

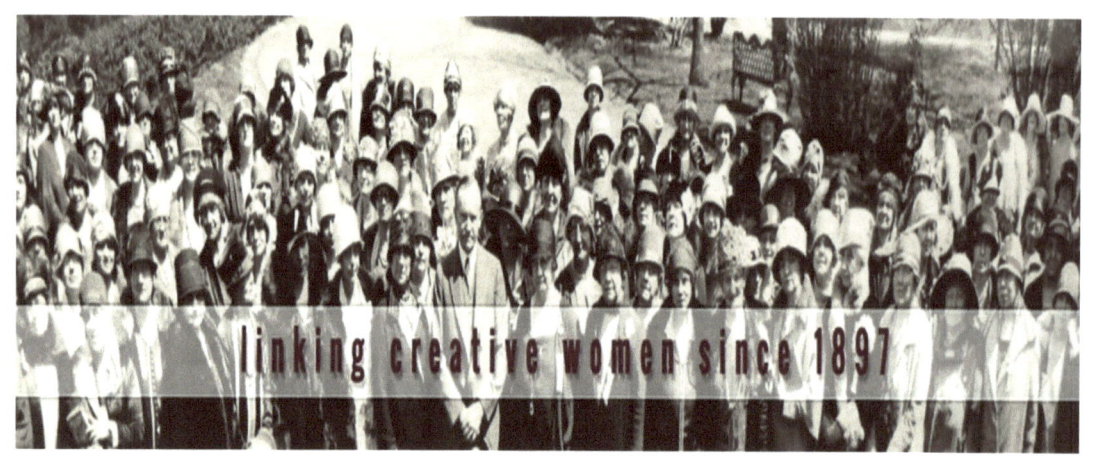

linking creative women since 1897

HISTORY

Pensacola Branch Turns 73

With 8 charter members, the Pensacola Branch of NLAPW began in April 1943. Officers of the newly-formed group were Miss Lola Lee Daniell, President; Miss Occie Clubbs, Recording Secretary (a teacher and principal for 48 years); Mrs. Frank Milner, Corresponding Secretary; and Mrs. Adrian Langford, Treasurer.

Current member Donna Freckmann remembers that she attended her first meeting in the mid 80s with her sponsor Autry Dye, a tea held in member Keets Rivers' home. Donna notes that the new president of the Florida National League would always begin her tour of the state in Pensacola, which was a big deal for a small chapter. Donna's first impression was one of a very genteel, gracious, intellectual, and talented group.

Now we have tripled our national membership in the last five years, and have included our many patrons in all our local activities. Led by our dynamic president Mara Viksnins, we meet once a month, usually at Artel Gallery, a beautiful art gallery in downtown Pensacola, sometimes at local restaurants.

Our meetings include poetry readings, show and tell, and a presentation by one of the members or a special guest. In addition to Mara, guiding us are our officers and board members: Vice President, Anne Baehr; Treasurer, Pam Wynn; Membership Chair, Autry Dye; Events Coordinators, Carol Loethen and Christine Salomé; Facebook and Technical Coordinator, Nancy Nesvik.

Our history is, of course, bound to the proud history of the National League of American Pen Women, founded in 1897 as a professional organization for women artists, composers, and writers. Branches throughout the U.S. offer seminars, workshops, art exhibits, readings, concerts, and outreach programs. Membership has many unique benefits at both the national and local levels. NLAPW membership provides the opportunity to network with other artists, enter national juried exhibits and contests, and participate in professional enrichment programs. Our Pensacola Branch proudly supports and contributes to the National goals and achievements.

Mara Viksnins, Anne Baehr, and Donna Freckmann contributed to this history.

ACKNOWLEDGEMENTS

This book would not have been possible without the hard work of Pensacola, Florida's National League of American Pen Women Branch Members and Patrons. Special gratitude is extended to Karen McAferty Morris and her colleague Mac McGovern, who worked many hours to organize, compile, and create our book. Our photographer Anne Baehr also played a dominant role in helping to facilitate professional photographic reproductions of our art. It was truly a labor of love and we will be indebted to them forever.

As our Pen Women chapter is more than seventy years old, we worked to create and record our time in this national organization and to perhaps extend its life for many, many more years in the future. It is part of our history as National League of Pen Women members.

Mara Viksnins, President

The Pensacola Branch, Mosaic by Anne Baehr

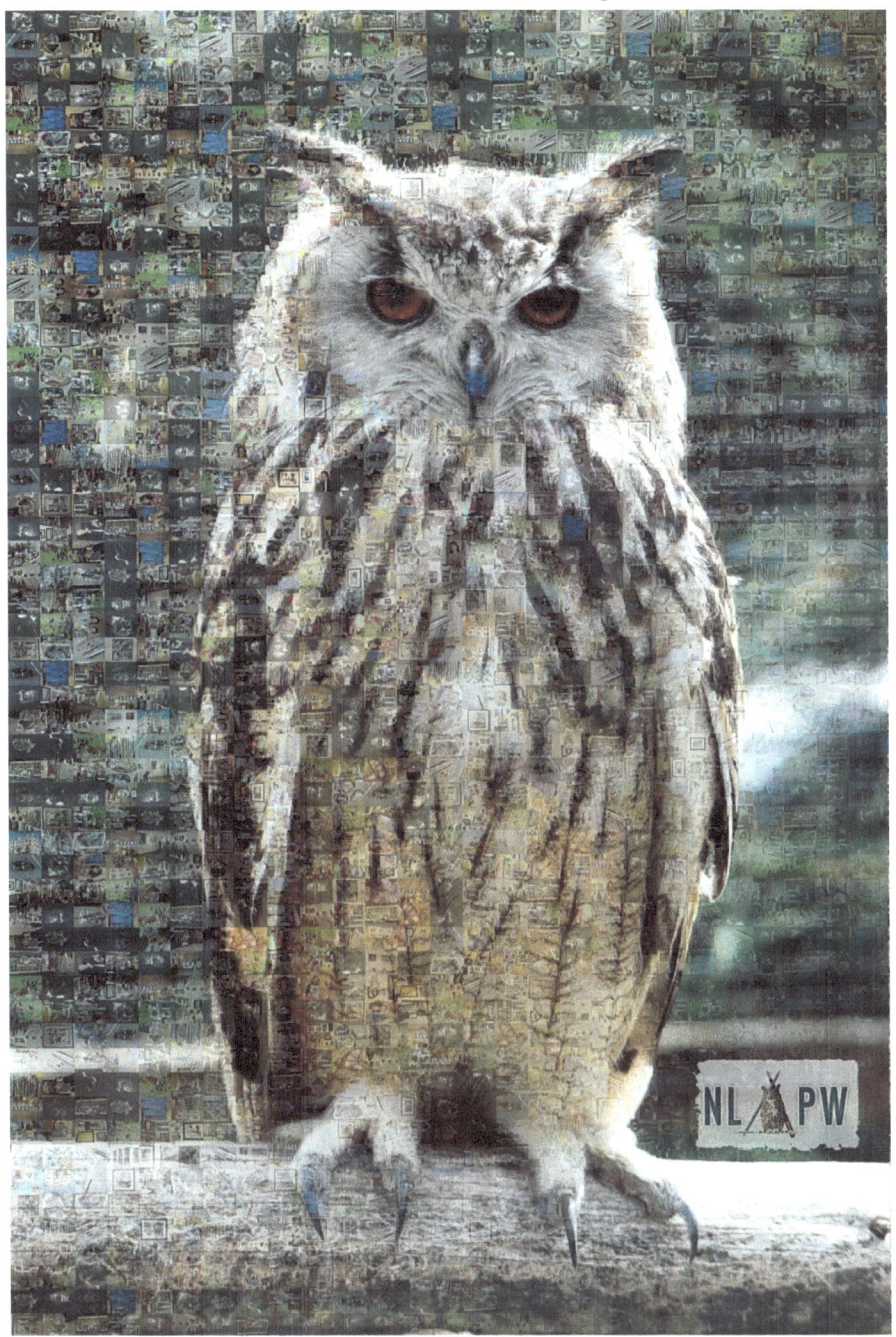

This photo mosaic by Anne Baehr named "The Pensacola Branch" represents our local branch of the National League of American Pen Women. This is representative of the broad range of talents of our artists, photographers, and writers, including watercolor, acrylics, scratch board, sculpting, fashion design, and collage. Our mission is to "encourage, recognize, and promote the production of creative work."

JANE C. NOWLIN
National Member

I love working. I love painting and drawing. I love color, form, design and compositional problems. I love meeting with friends to paint even if they do not share my views on what constitutes art. Most of them are modernists and I am not. I use my studio nearly every day for one reason or another. Sometimes to paint, sometimes to plan, sometimes to read. My outlook on life is sunny, so my art is considered sunny, high key, and happy. I leave it to others to be shocking or avant guard, or boldly crass. I don't even mind it being called feminine or saccharine. I'm too old "to fight the good fight" of whether or not a 340-ton rock is art, or if a man squatting to defecate is worthy of being in a major museum. You the viewers are free to judge for yourselves.

I've studied art in one way or another for over 50 years, in books, DVD's, and in hundreds of conversations with wonderful artist acquaintances. I studied formally in private lessons with Rubye Briden in Dallas whenever I could afford them. I've taken many workshops, most recently with Charles Reid, Janet Rogers, and Don Andrews. Workshops are now my favorite way to study and be introduced to new and exciting ways to apply paint.

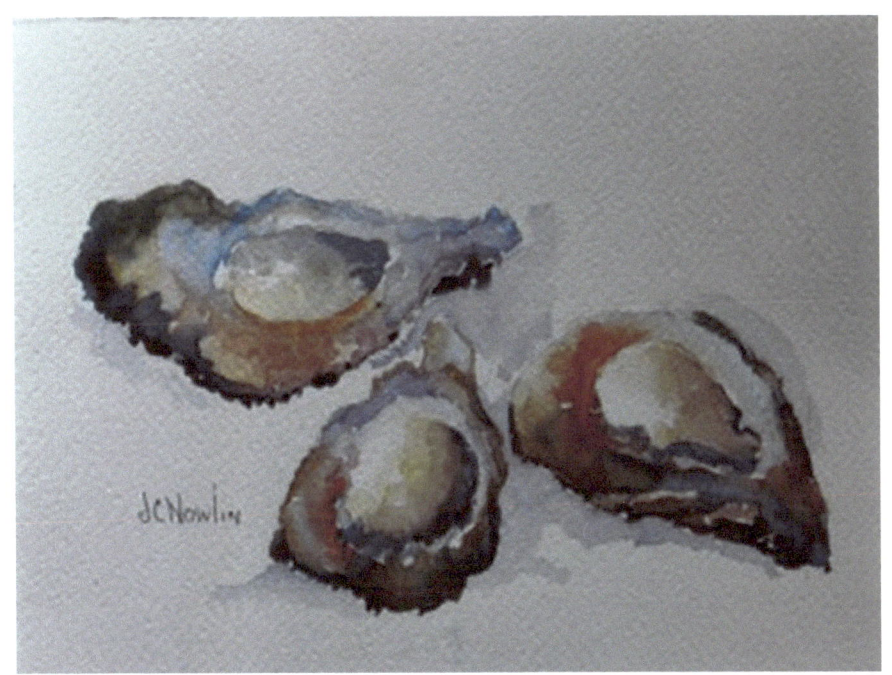

Apalachicola Prize

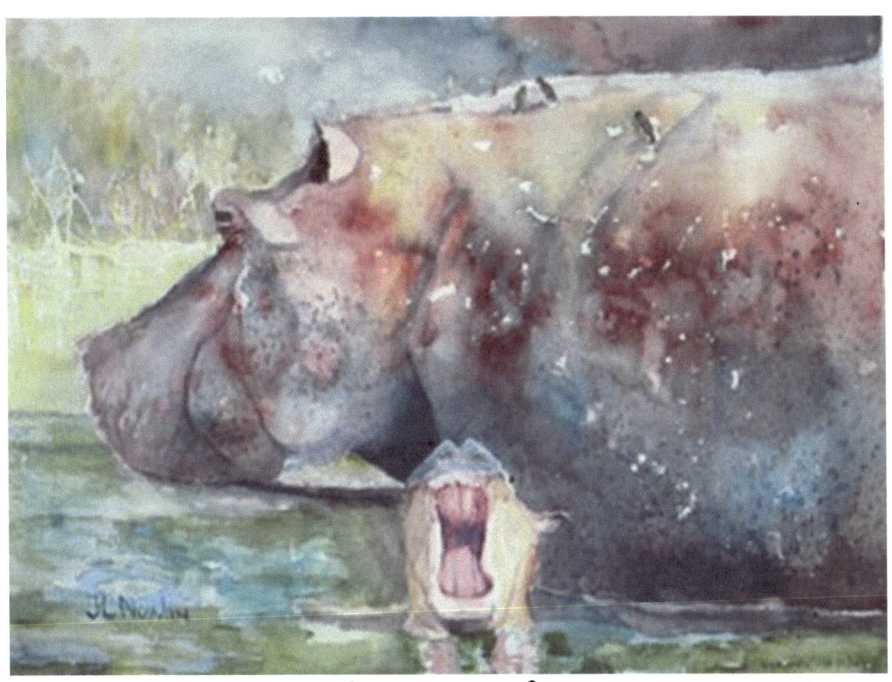

Danger Lurks

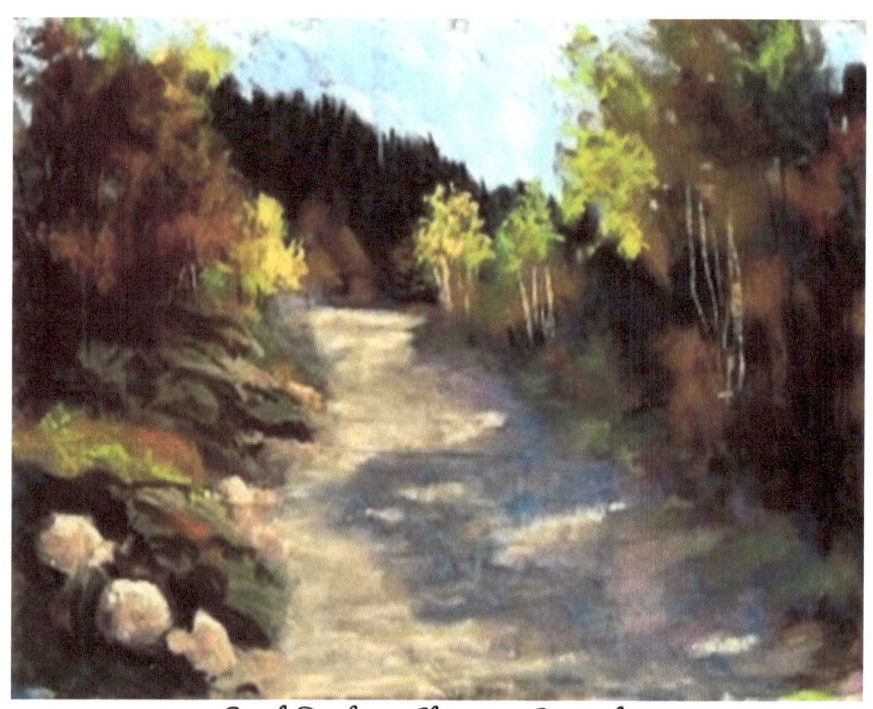

South Dakota Elegance Everywhere

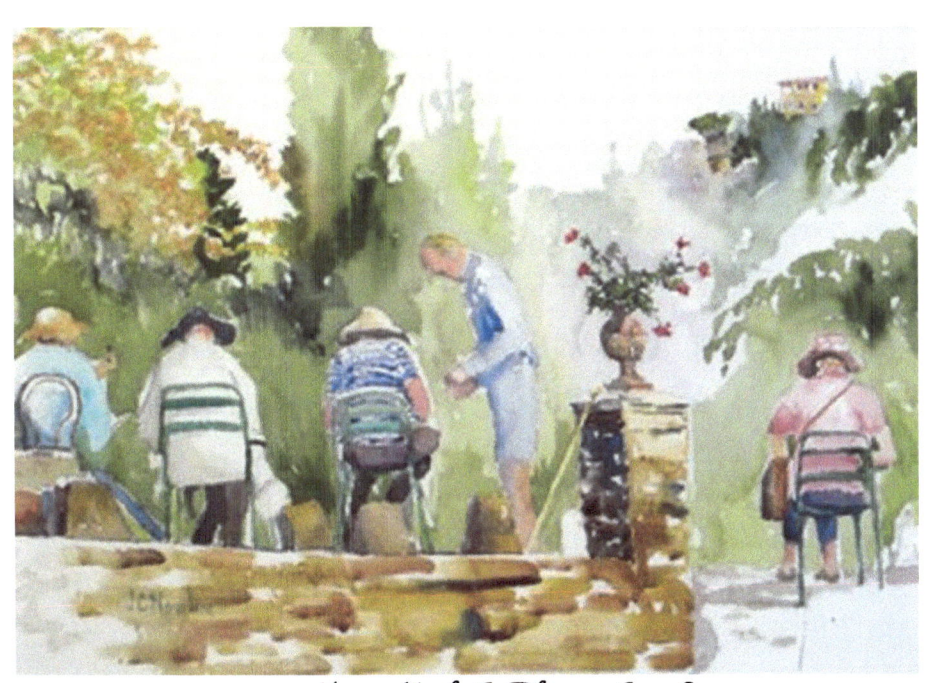

How Much Is That in Euros?

CAROL LOETHEN, EVENTS COORDINATOR
National Member

I am a self-taught artist who doesn't seem to follow the "rules." I seem to follow an experimental approach to my work. So when Ever'man's Natural Foods here in Pensacola asked artists to provide green art for Earth Day, I was excited, and was honored to win Best Medium for the piece of work titled "Gruner Tag." I have learned over the years that my art reflects my love for fashion. Letting the experience of creation guide me, I decided to try my hand using mixed media. I had no clear vision of how the piece would present itself but decided to experiment with watercolor paints, inks, and various mediums.

I had recently traveled to Italy, and while at the airport in Germany I picked up a fashion magazine. I cut out the beautiful German typography from its pages, and tea stained them. I used these tea-stained pages as the backdrop for this new piece of art. Dipping my brush in India ink, I then randomly sketched a woman onto the background, and then added touches of watercolor paint in green and pink to her face. Since I find beauty in textures, I create using found or discarded items as my inspiration. I formed a dress using strips of recycled fabric in greens and blues, then outlined and accented using black India ink. The name for this art could only be "Gruner Tag," which is German for Green Day.

At one of our NLAPW meetings we were challenged to do a piece of work from a poem. I chose a poem titled "Harvest Moon," written by one of our talented Pen Women, Jane Lies. I love fashion, so I started my vision by drawing a woman's face using pencils and watercolor.

I have been told that this illustration looks very similar to me. I guess I really put myself into my art. I then took this fashion illustration and enhanced it on the computer. Each eye is a photo of the moon that I took while on a cruise along the Mexican Riviera. I love the depth that this added to my art. I titled it "Moon in Her Eyes." This piece was juried into Artel Gallery's "Go Show," March 10 – April 17, 2015. I was also thrilled and honored to sell my art piece during this show. Each piece I create reflects my passion and love for art.

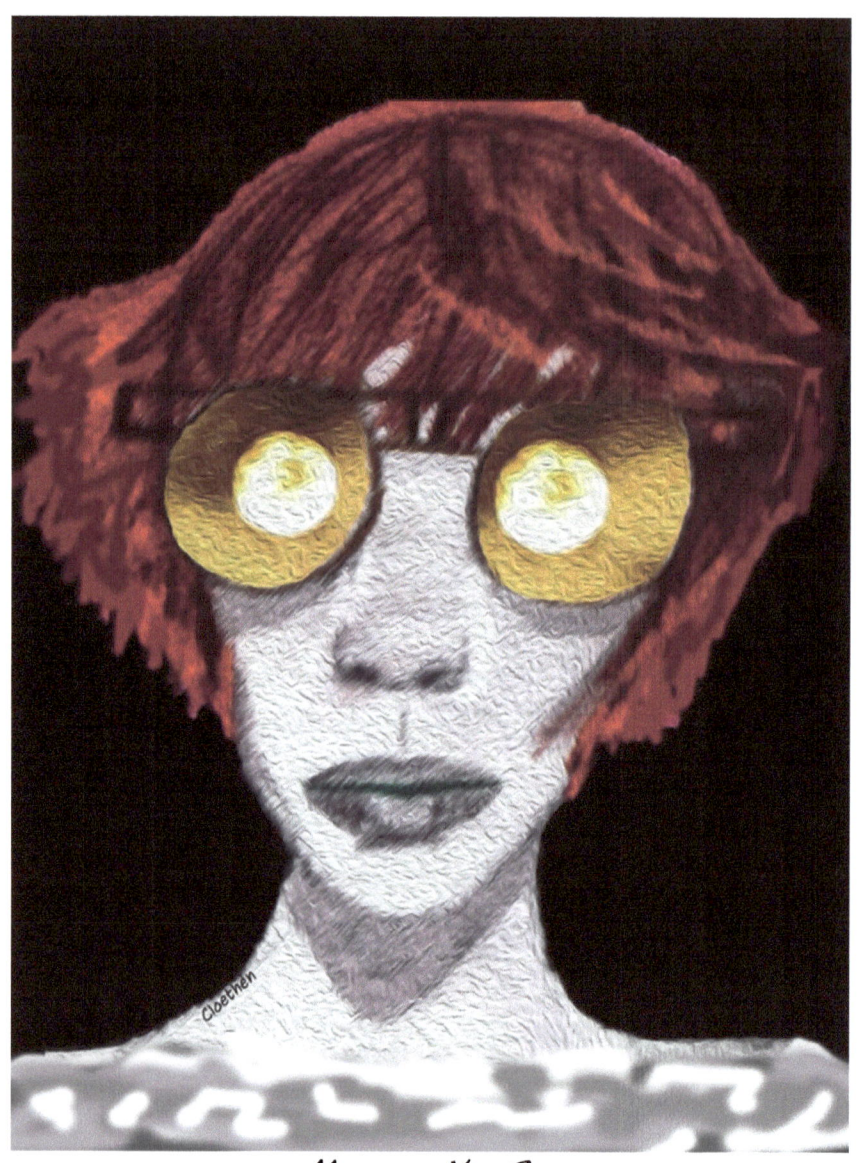

Moon in Her Eyes

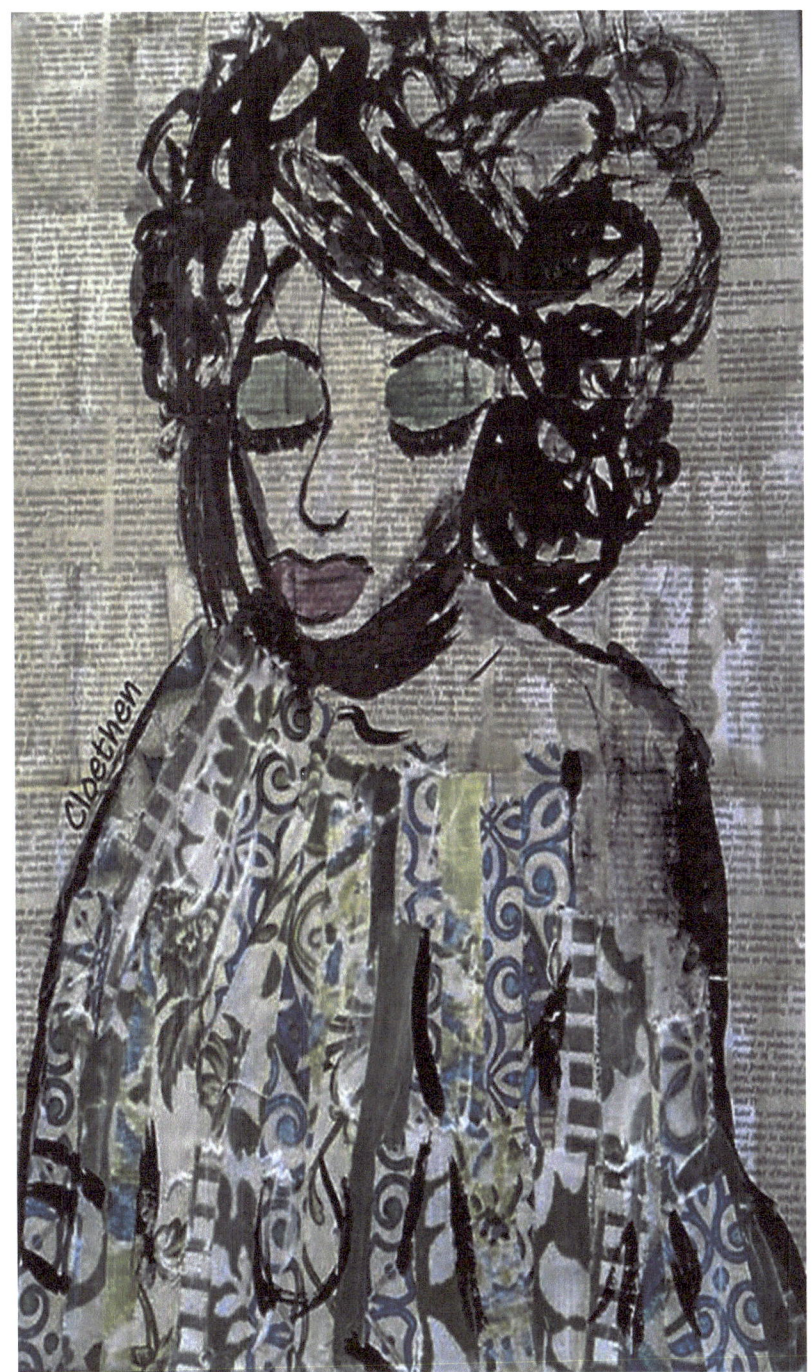

Gruner Tag

JANE G. LIES
National Member

When an idea comes to me for a painting or for a passage in my writing, I feel that I transition silently toward another dimension. I love painting. What comes forth from me onto the canvas is something very private. Initially, my hands work without much thought to get the outline or the idea to flow; then my hands work together with my imagination to make the work visible. I have no particular style. My impulse leads me toward a myriad of subjects: flowers, landscapes, portraits. As in my writing, I never know what will be next. I do know that my work will generally not be in the abstract or non-objective. I paint representationally, in that I paint pretty much what I see, albeit I do take artistic license to make the subject matter work artistically on canvas. For instance, I might make a background blue instead of green if I feel the painting needs the change.

I love color and I am less concerned with form unless I am working on a portrait. I often enjoy drawing with a pencil – any kind of pencil. My pencil drawings are usually small and very often I draw to study the construction of a piece. I also enjoy working with oils, watercolor and pastels.

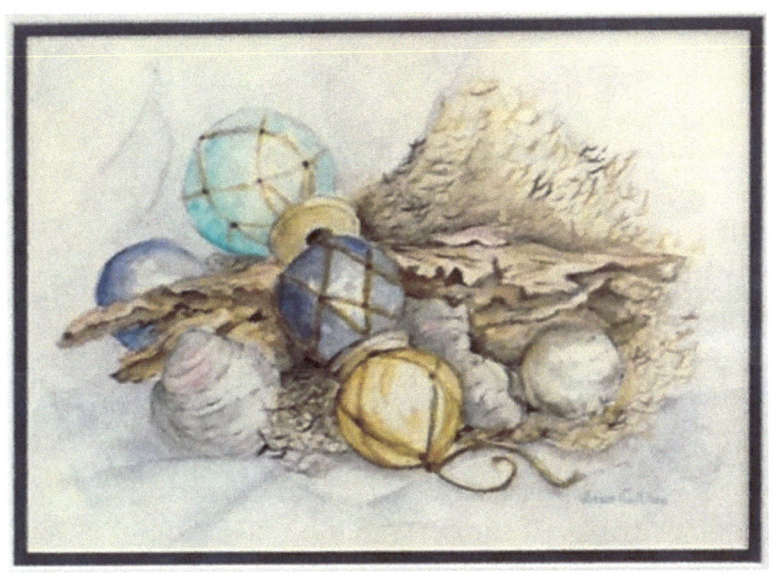

Seaside

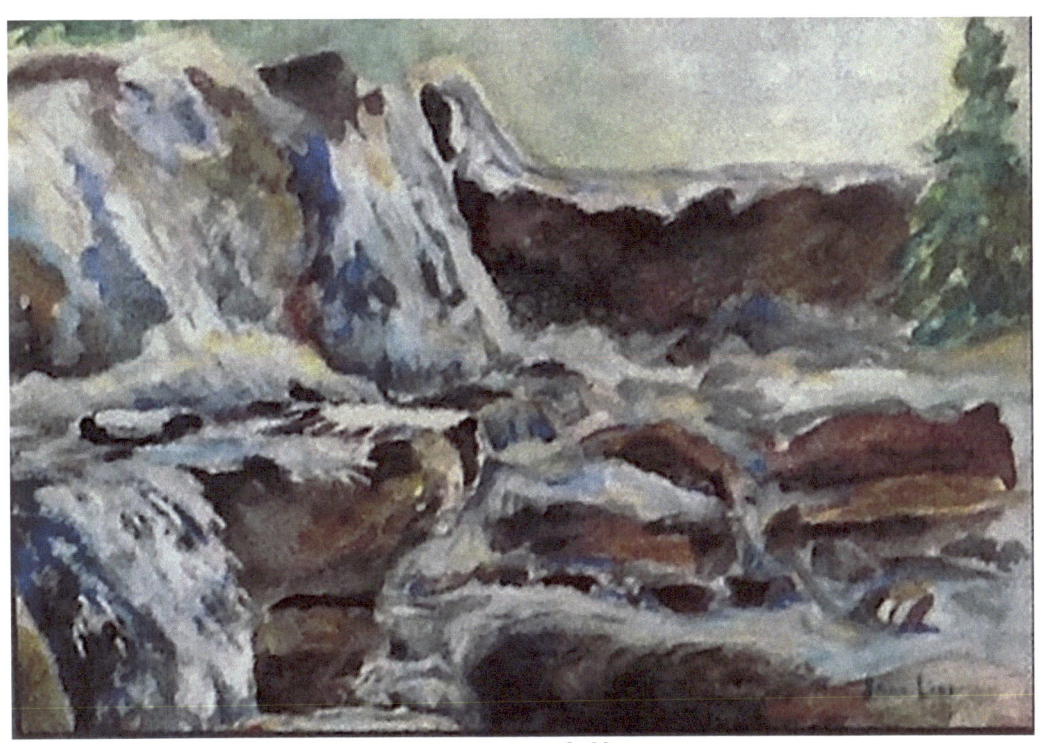

Waterfall

The Rose

Morning shadows wash gracefully
Over imperfect gray concrete,
A gentle breeze wakes the rose
From its midnight nap,
To new splendor,

A cat sleeping among the leaves
Surveys the dawn,
Then moves skillfully through
The connected knots of nature's rope,
A jungle of stems and thorns,

A lizard scampers nearby, noticed
By the awakened cat,
A circular movement of the lizard's tail
Blends into the sienna of darkness,
Rocks and sticks are the lizard's friend,

With unseen orders,
Ants follow in a soldier's line,
As a bee buzzes nearby alone,
Lighting softly on one red petal,
A perfect choice,

The dance continues,
Until total darkness fills all vacant space,
Under the watchful moon,
Once again,
All living things sleep,

The heart beats in many places in the dark,
Always in its own entity,
The shadow sleeps beneath the rose bush,
Silently, hidden in sleep until tomorrow,
When life begins again.

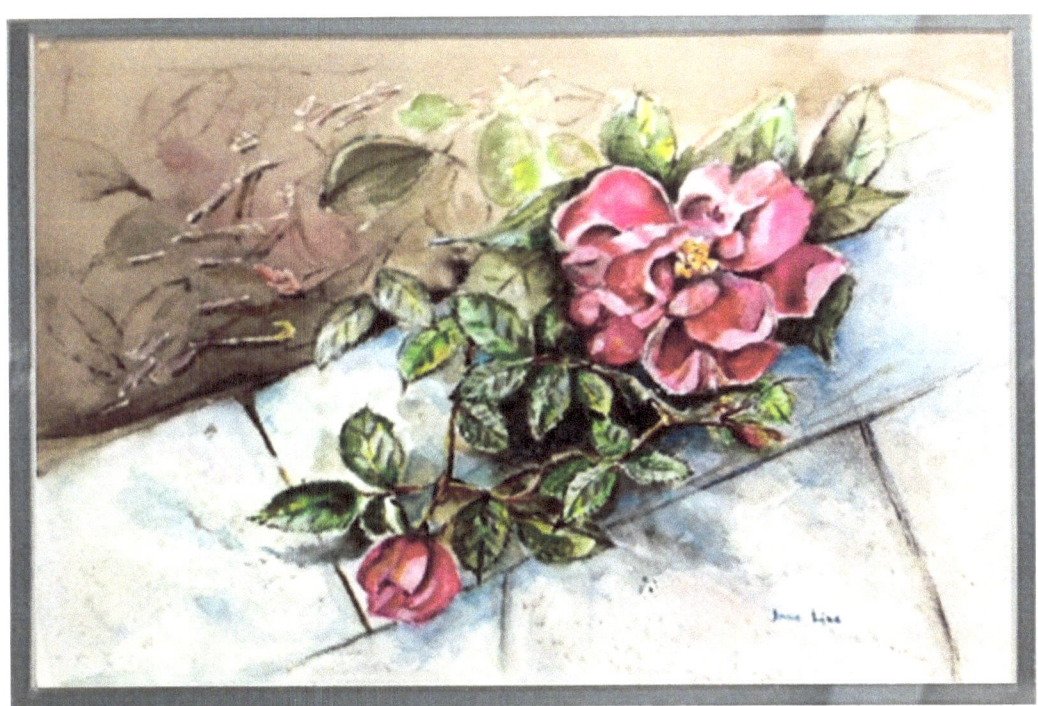

Rose

ANNE BAEHR, VICE PRESIDENT
National Member

I love photography and am consumed with photographing people as attractively and authentically as possible. In my artistic endeavors, I portray my subjects in a truthful way, but aim to capture the viewer's attention by using unique photographic styles: mosaics, collage, abstract photographs, and painted effects to capture the imagination.

A quote from Ansel Adams, "You don't take a photograph, you make one," inspires me to take my photography a step further and create digital art out of my pictures.

What started out as a hobby photographing butterflies at different stages of development became a creative journey of making a mosaic titled "Metamorphosis," which won first place in Photography at the National League of American Pen Women Biennial meeting in Washington, D.C., 2012.

My experimental photograph "Optical Aberration" is considered a one of a kind prismatic art and received the Judge's Award at the 2014 Cinco Banderas Show at Artel Gallery in Pensacola, FL.

"One Last Look," a collage, takes the viewer on a woman's life journey by using a cracked looking glass to display periods of her life. By using this effect, attention is captured as viewers question "What has happened to her?" It won first place in the 2014 Homage to the Past Show at Artel Gallery. "Caught by Surprise" was inspired by a video clip of my granddaughter getting caught by a rogue wave at Pensacola Beach, destroying her sandcastle and drenching her on a cool November day. By layering the blue watercolor background first and then incorporating the photograph onto it, the scene was recreated on paper. Another artistic puzzle solved. It was exhibited in the Power of Photography Show at the Pensacola Museum of Art, 2015.

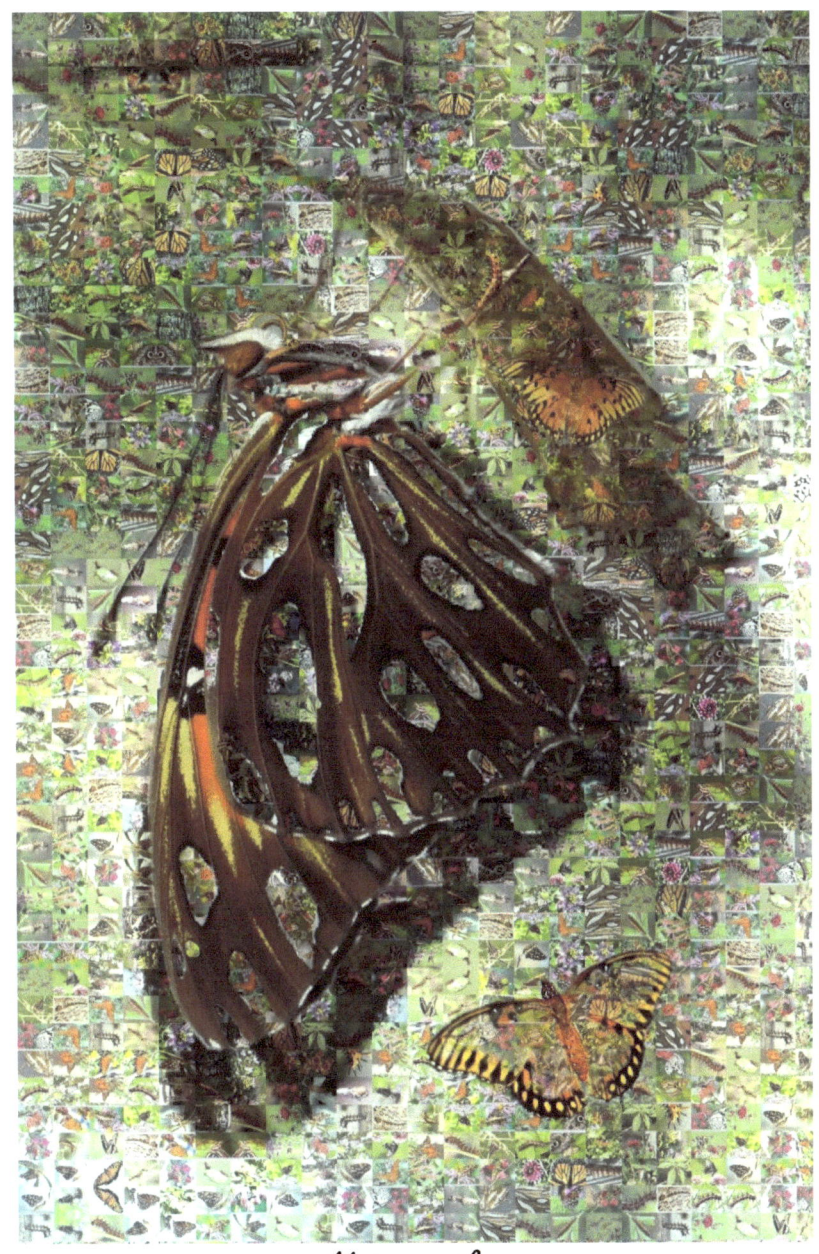

Metamorphosis

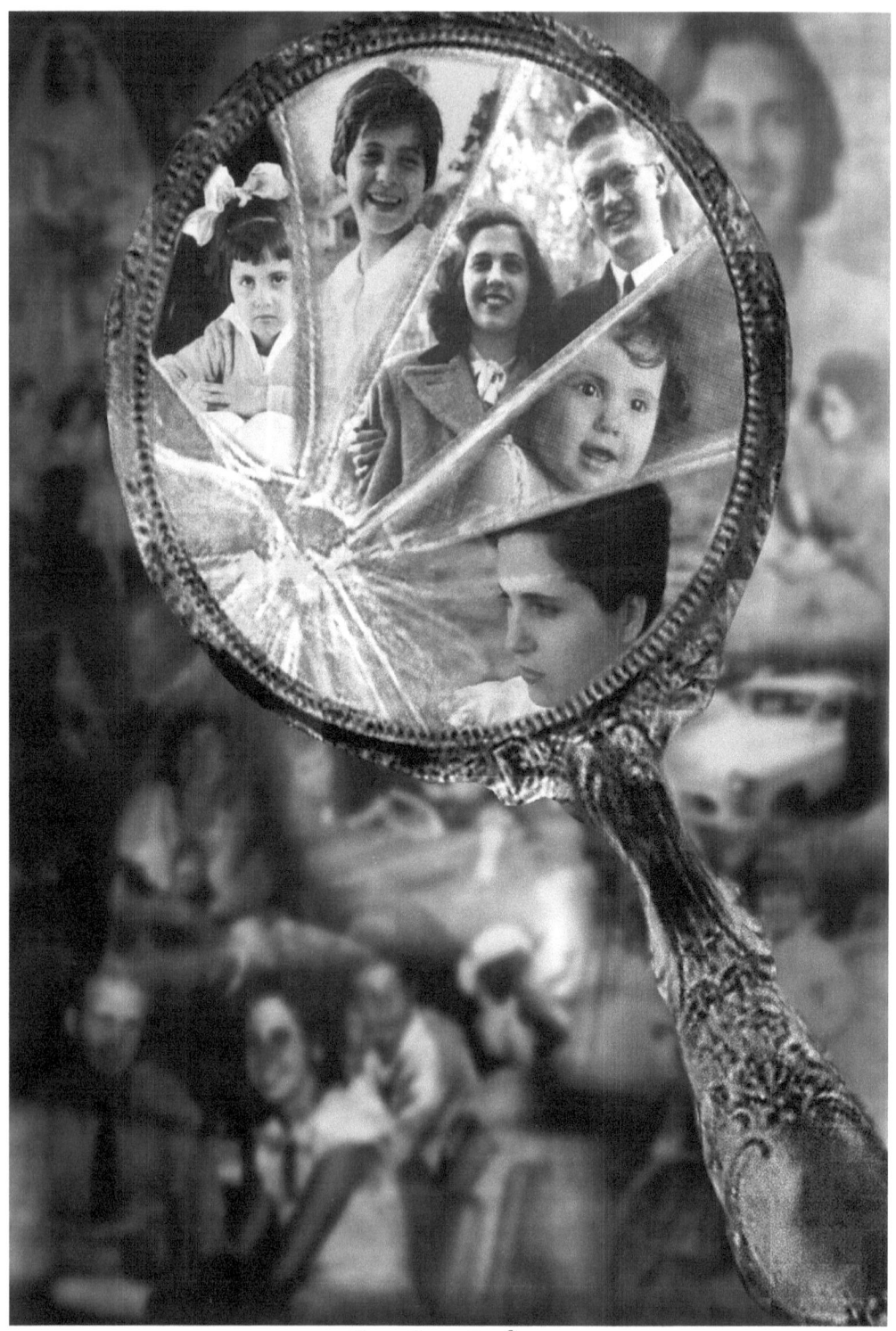

One Last Look

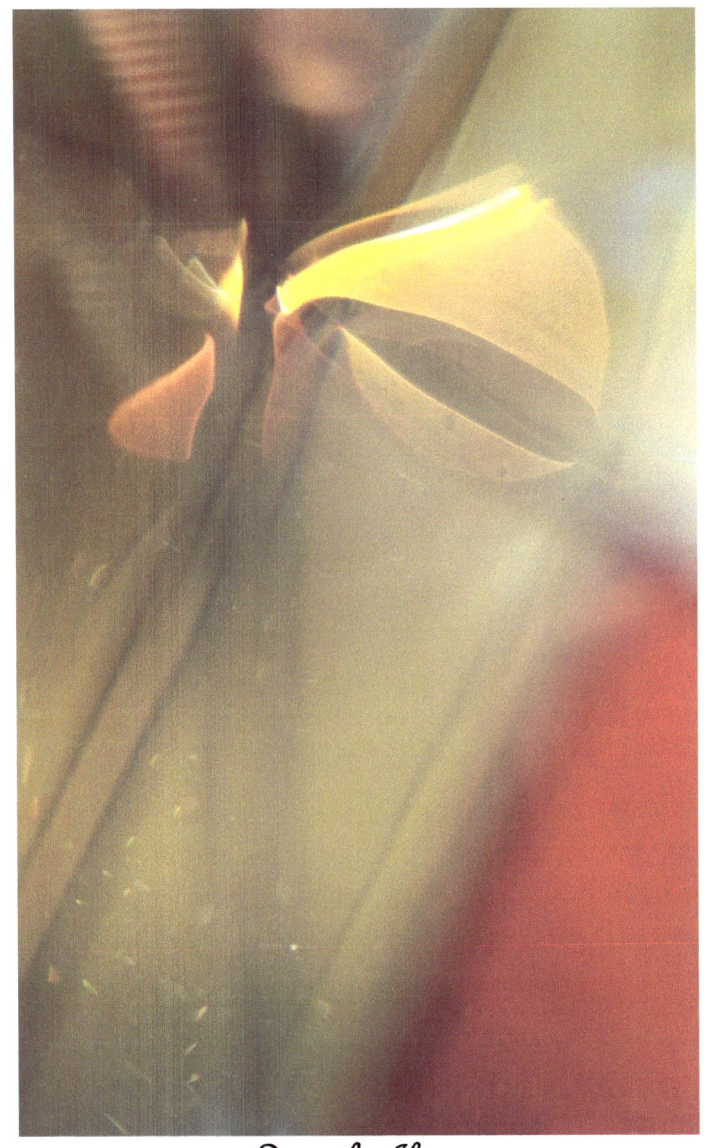

Optical Aberration

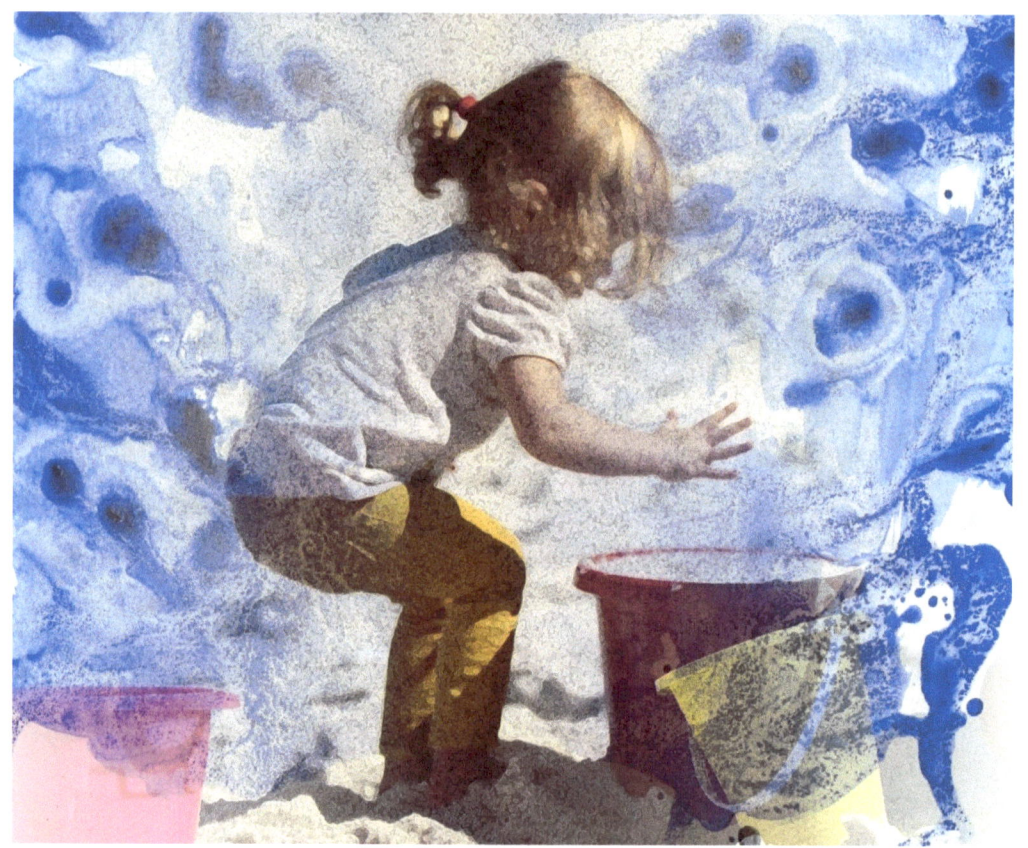

Caught by Surprise

KAREN BICKNELL
National Member

At an early age I was introduced to the enchantment of the forests in northern Wisconsin. Our lake cabin surrounded by birch and aspen trees became my setting for storytelling through my artwork. I used animals to carry the narrative.

In my paintings, animals join us in our living space through whimsical brushwork. Is it nature or humanity itself that is meeting our own gaze in a playful way? "Bear Catch," painted in watercolor, was designed to be viewed at eye level. Collectors of my work often wonder if this is an animal or a human being portrayed enjoying the sport. What I imply heavily in my work is that there is no hierarchy in our world. We are all on the same level and all share in this experience together. I encourage everyone to reflect in the muse of wildlife and simply enjoy.

That is why I paint. Art sends my message.

Other favorite subject matters of mine are landscapes in abstract design painted in watercolor or acrylic over gold leaf that tie me back to my origins. The outside world has come inside and has its own life in refractive light play.

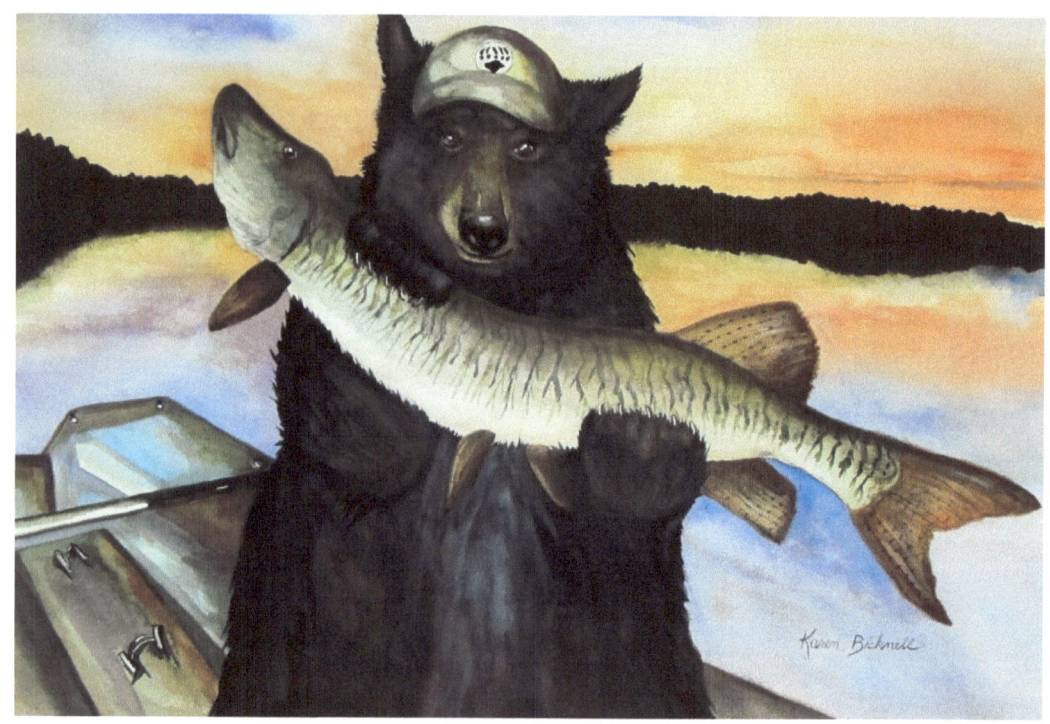

Bear Catch

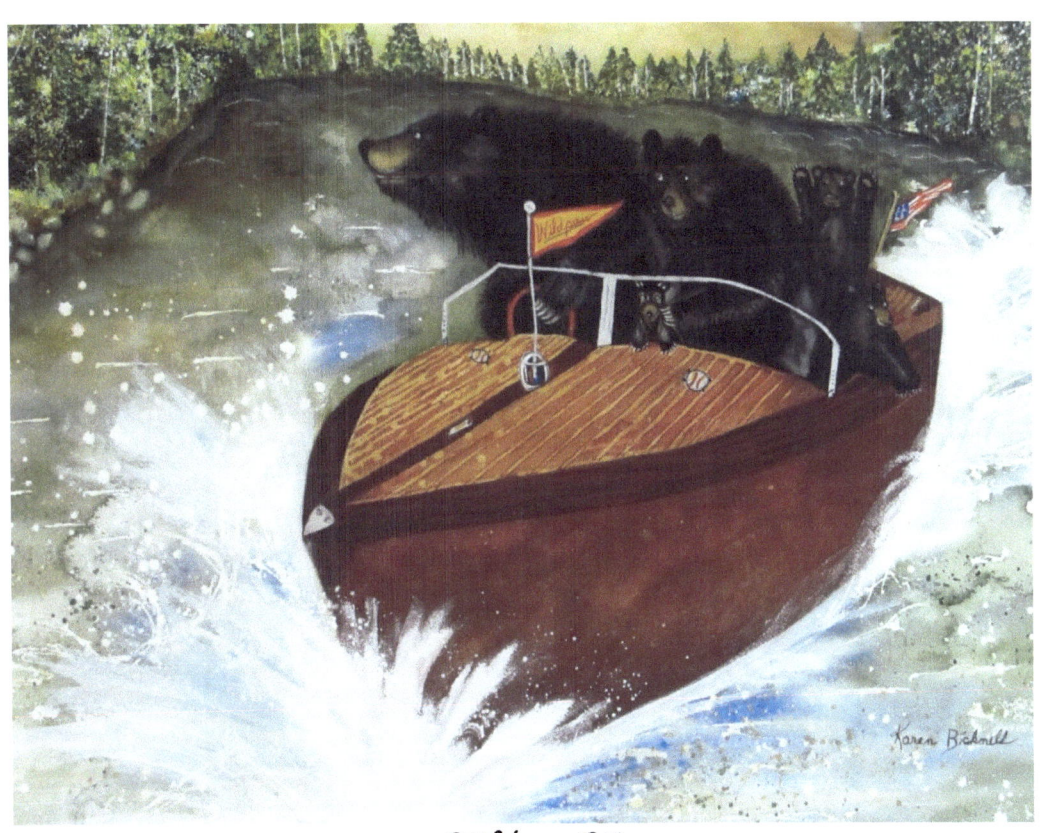

Wildpaw Waves

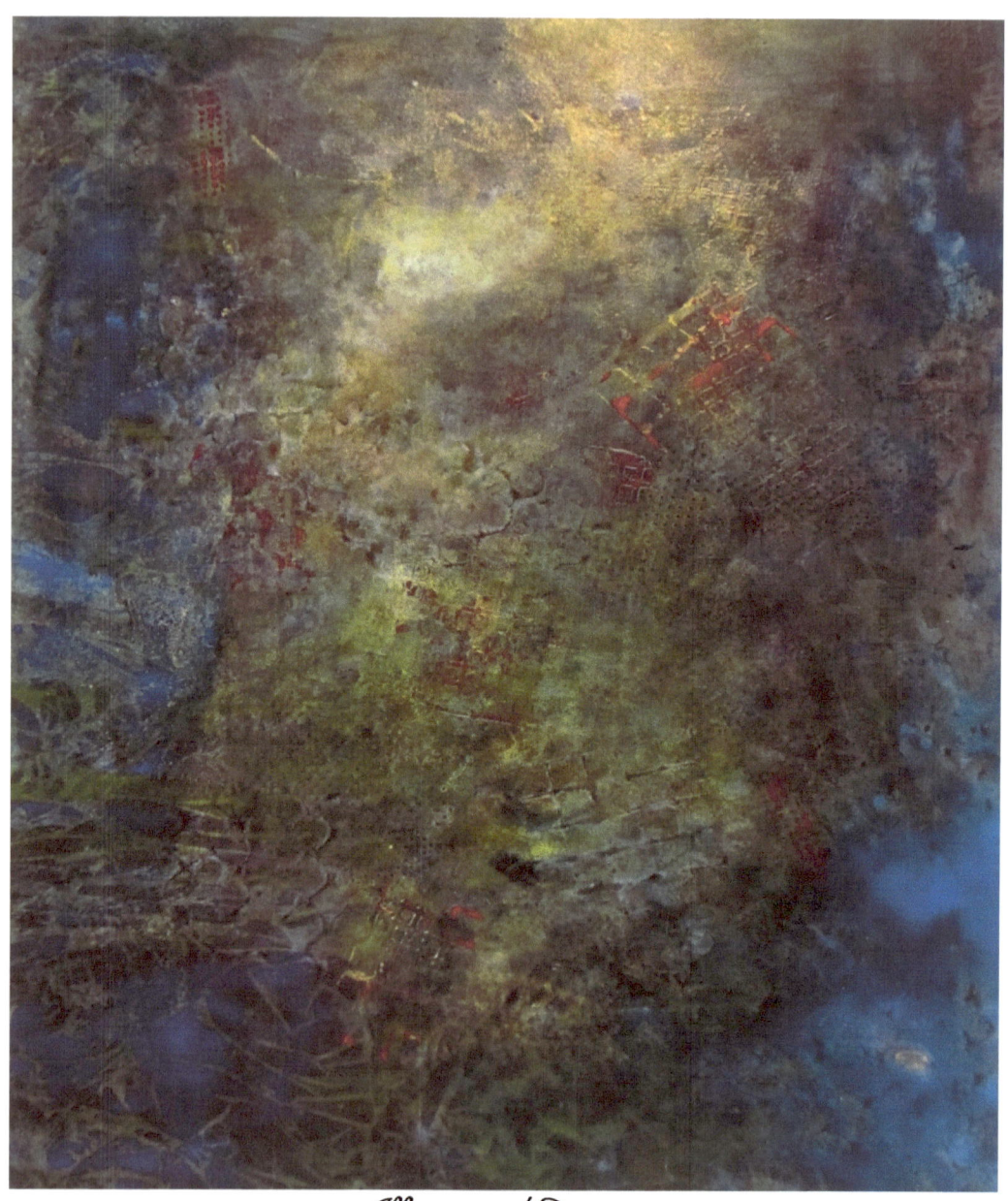

Illuminated Dance

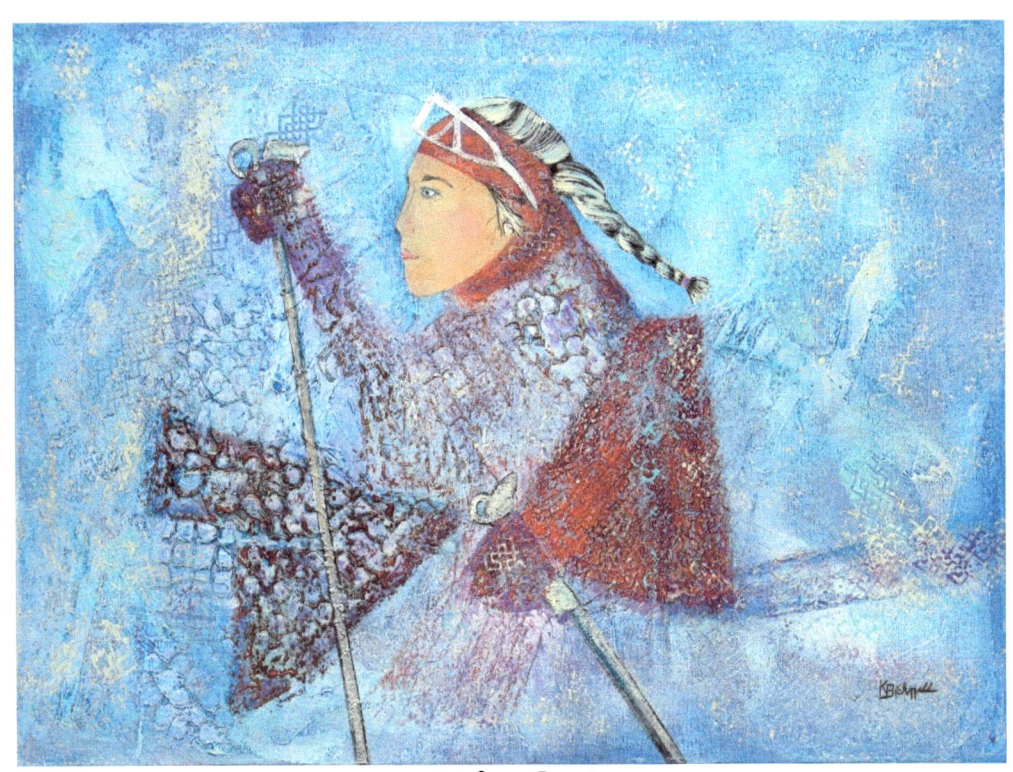

The Race

DIANA KAYE OBE

I have created art in one form or another from the time I was a small child, molding images in the mud, and later working in a taxidermy shop of an internationally known bronze artist and taxidermist during high school. I cannot imagine life without making art. I have used as many mediums as possible, but primarily stay with acrylic and oil painting, and charcoal. Oil is my favorite because of the depths of the colors and my admiration of the old masters.

I find beauty in faces and people, no matter the age. Although I have a broad range of subjects I work with, portraits are my favorite subject. It really depends on my spiritual space at the time. Many times I paint dreams, just "things and ideas in my head." Still life holds an attraction for me as I think, other than landscapes, one can delve deeply into light, shape, translucencies, design, and depth.

Hopefully I will be still doing art in my centenarian years.

The Gift

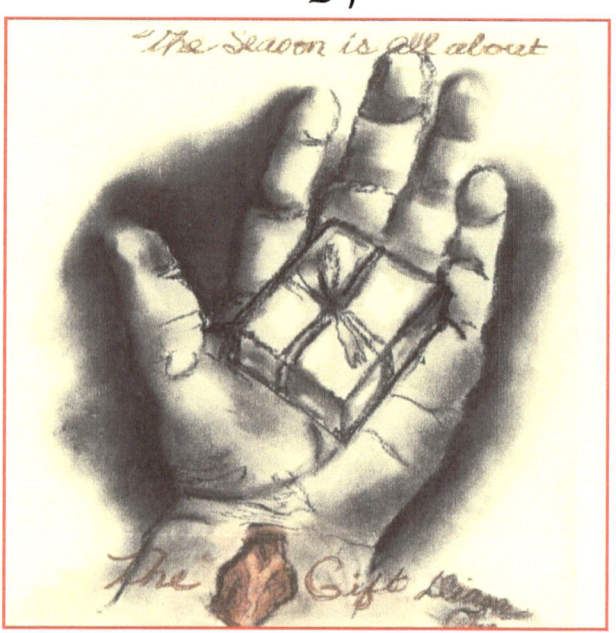

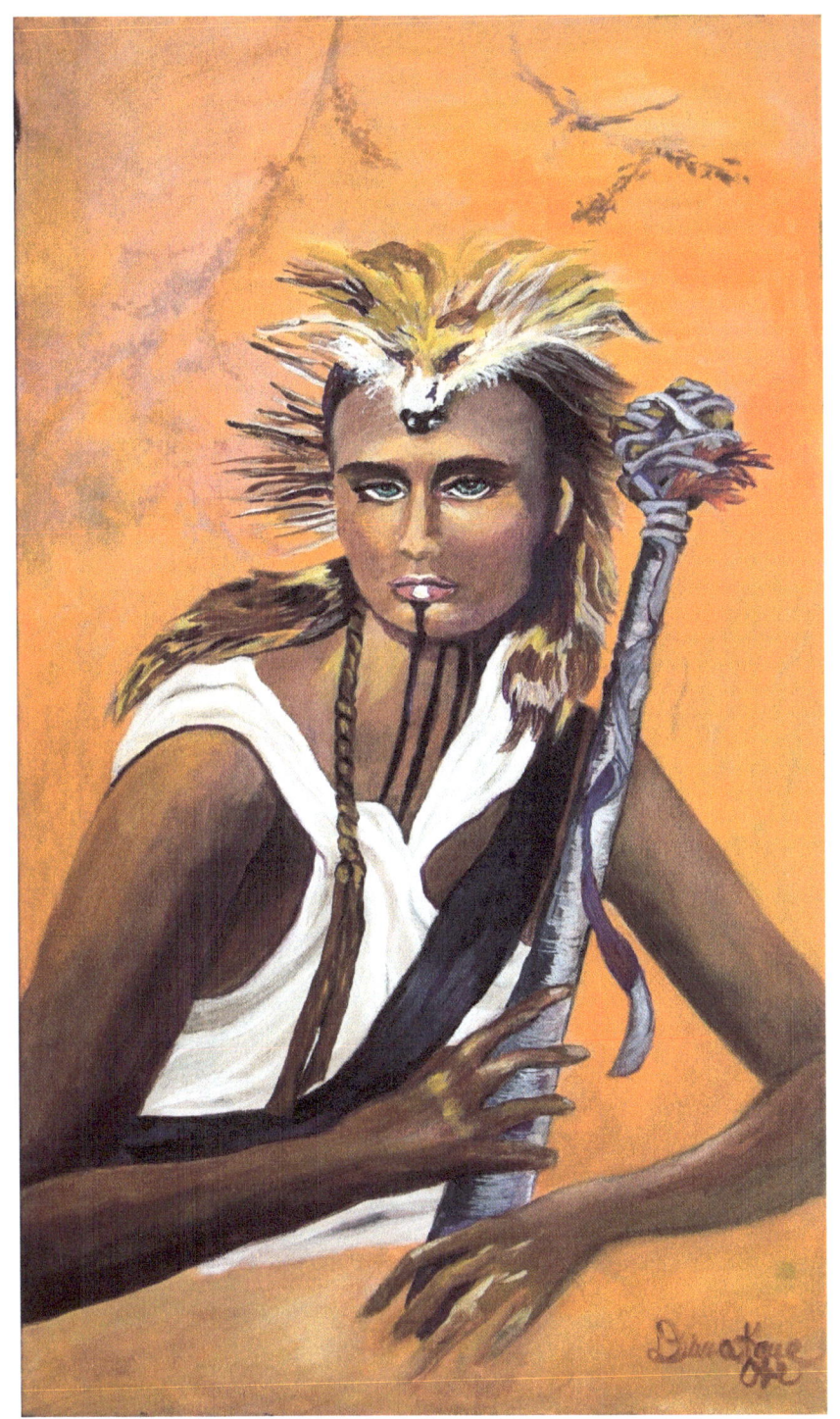

Warrior Woman

The Savior

In velvety black night Mary sat
Looking up at the stars
And bemused considered the
State of where her life was at.

A promise of greatness beyond
Her imagination lay under her belly
Wrapped sarong, "Just tell me, God,
Will his life be short or long?"

As the child came and then grew
Mary, remembering prophesy old,
Looked at the reality of life
And a shadow crossed her, cold.

A babe, a child, a man,
Then the times of trouble began,
Many times resolute he stood against the crowd
As they cursed him with epithets loud.

It seemed that no matter who believed and heard
The healings brought hatred as well as joy
And often Mary's eyes filled with tears
As she remembered her dear little boy.

The time came, his seriousness grew,
Her heart tormented with what she foreknew;
They came and tore him from place of prayer,
All she could do was pray and follow him there.

Each spike in his body entered her heart,
A piece tore from her soul as up went the cross.
Wildly she prayed, frantically she schemed,
"Stop, oh stop, for him this is not what I've dreamed!"

She stood at the foot of the cross.
As his body died, her soul sank in death too.
Her knees no longer held her up
As she sank in despair, "Oh, God, why so much loss?"

God was silent as the sky eerily darkened,
Clouds rolled as if heaven were in torment too.
Even the mockers shivered in fear
And then, "It is done."

Mary, mind numbed by grief, old prophecies
Nearly forgotten, aided by John
Looked up with bewildered eyes,
"Where has my baby gone?"

Reality settled in. Yes, He was gone,
Many walked about stunned, where was their song?
Then soon He appeared, to the women only,
"Mama don't weep, I promise you'll never be lonely."

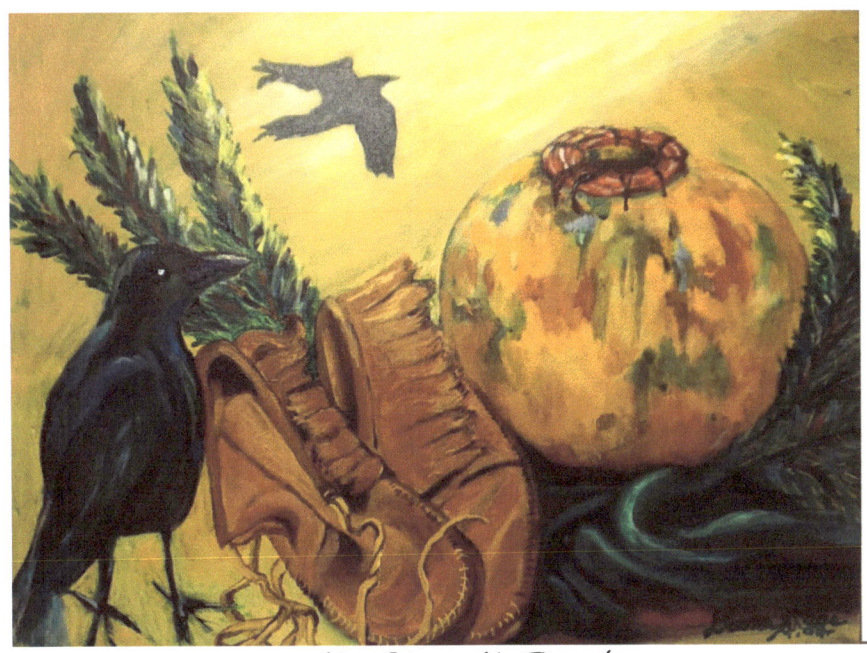

Miss You, My Friend

HELEN BRETON

In 1995 I started painting exclusively with watercolor. I took weekly private lessons for over three years. I thoroughly enjoyed painting regularly in a small group. Although I am a naturally creative person, being in a group forced me to exercise that creativity.

I enjoy both plein air and studio painting, and have been fortunate enough to plein air paint on beautiful Monhegan Island in Maine.

I have recently started working with acrylic paint, which is a total change from watercolors. Luckily there are mediums and additives that have been developed that allow the user to work at a slow pace, making the process more enjoyable.

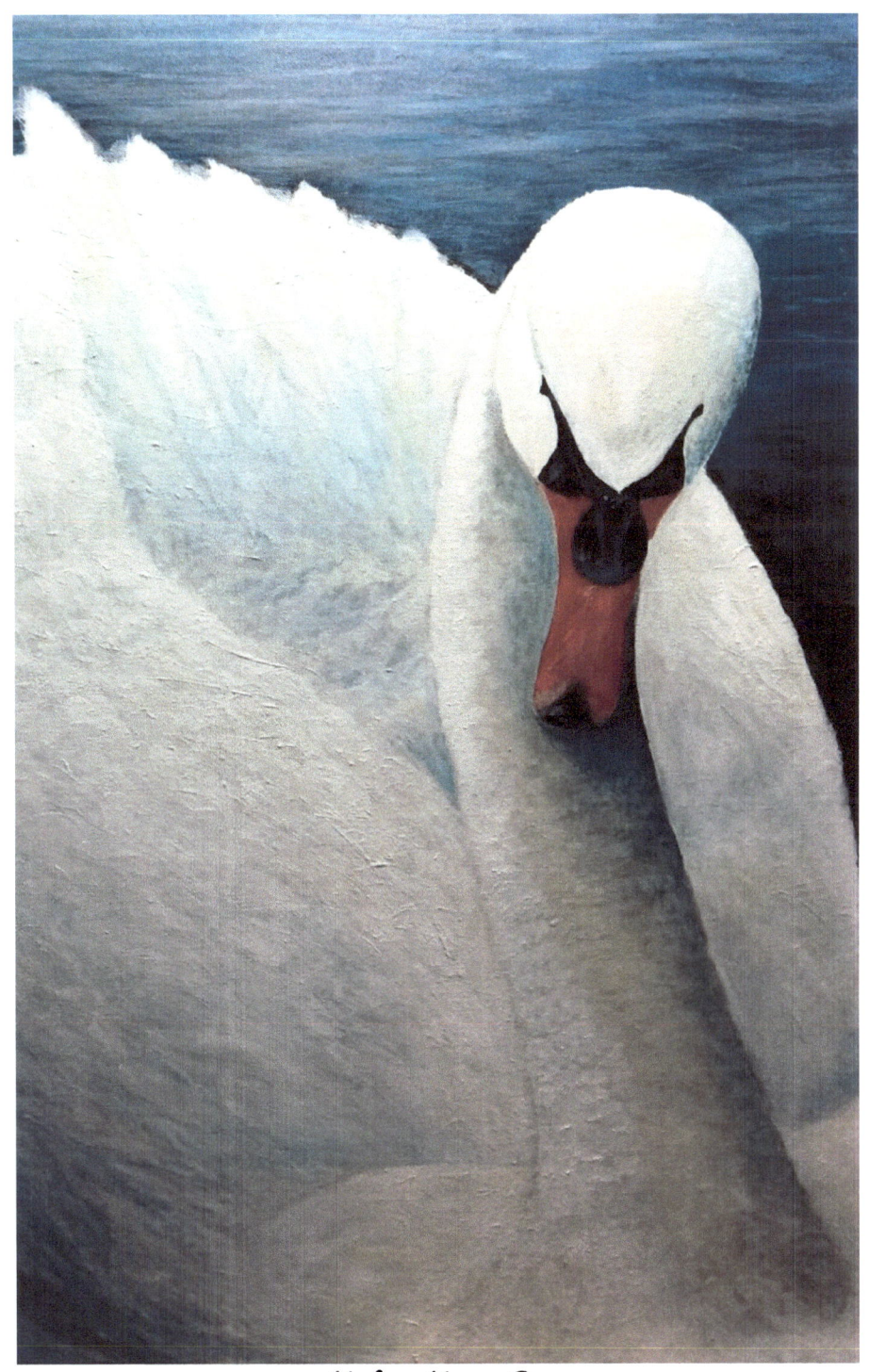

Male Mute Swan

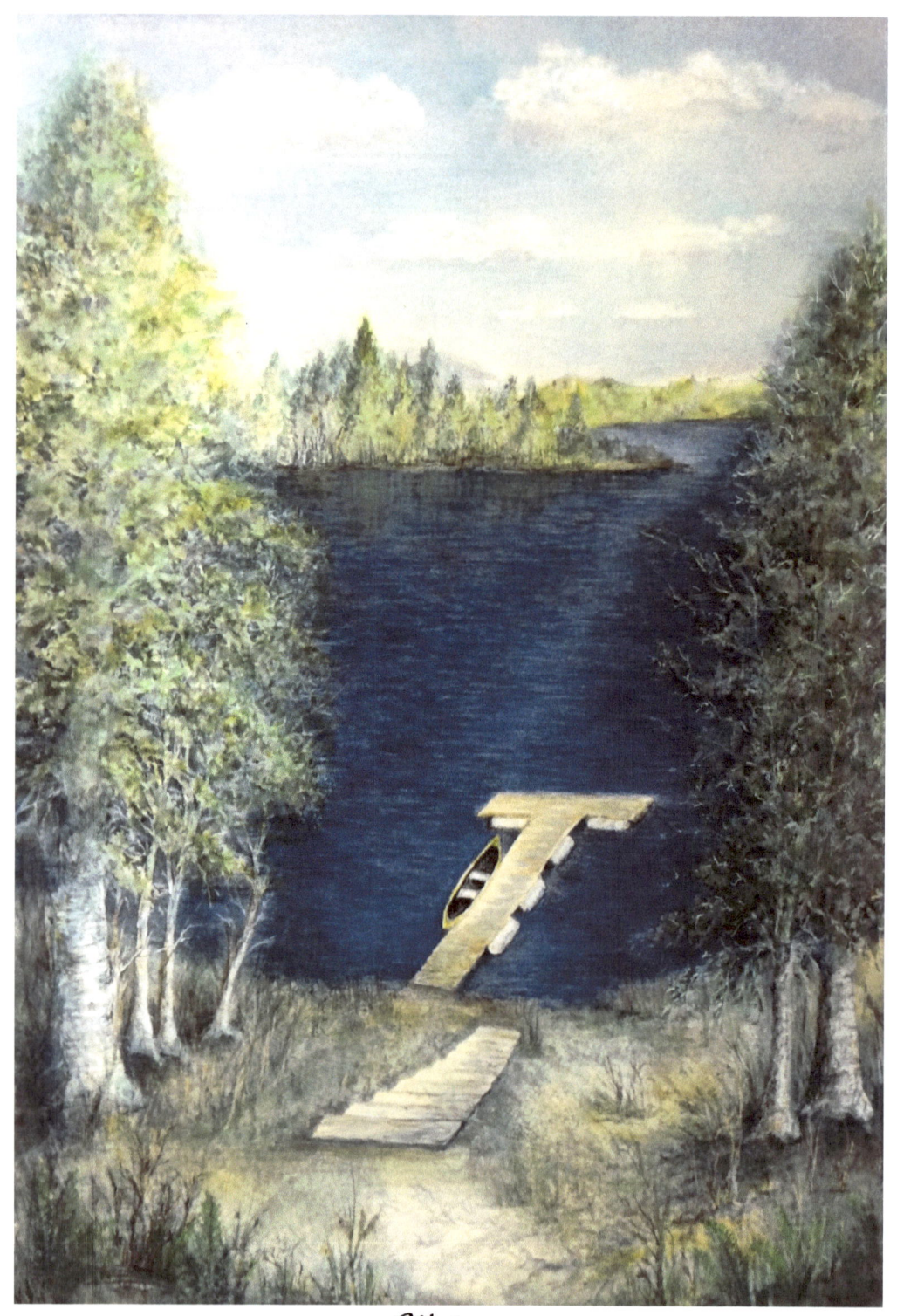

Waiting

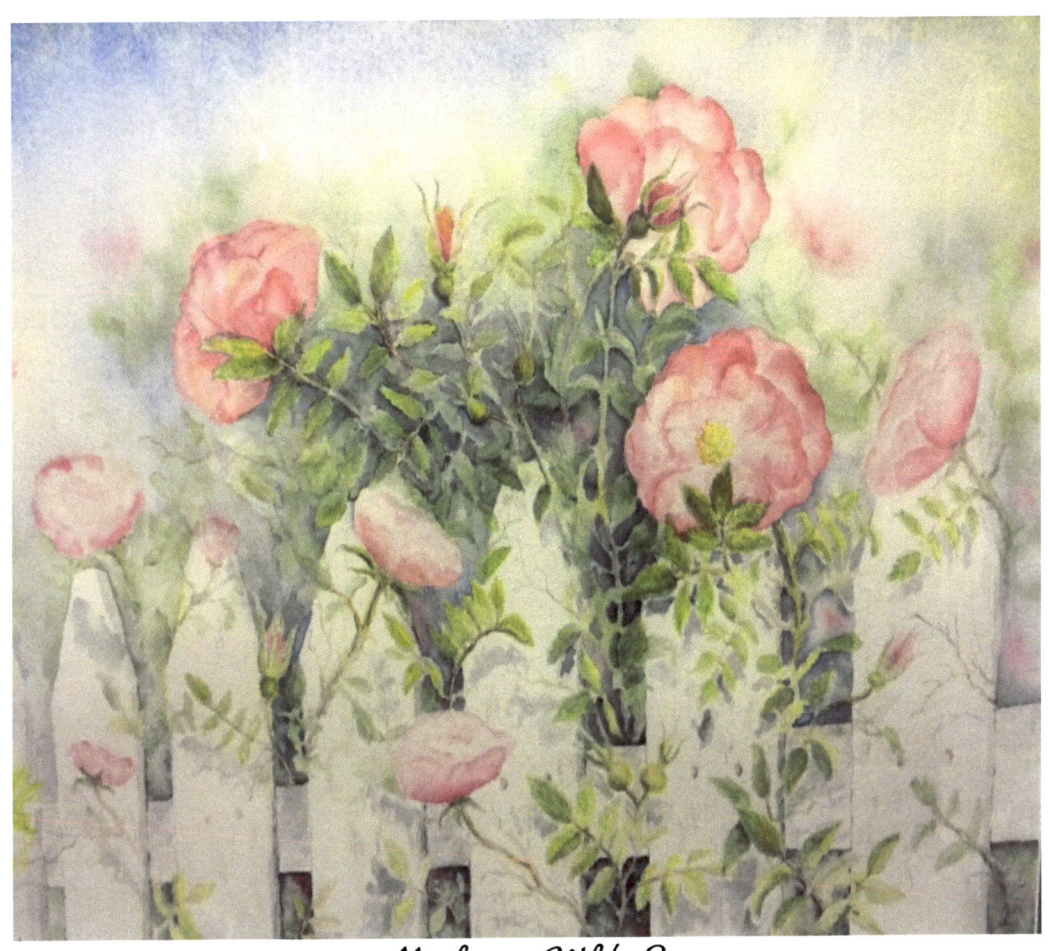

Monhegan Wild Rose

MAGGI DIERCKS ROBERTS
National Member

Technically flawless. Compositionally compelling. Cognizant of the *WOW* factor to evoke an emotional response. Style. Subject. Presentation. Story Telling. These are the elements that define that perfect photo according to the Professional Photographers Association.

Sometimes I think it isn't about how we shoot or what we shoot with after all, but what we see and feel with it post-processing. The *Art* lies in what our images say to us, and that can vary with those that view it! For me, capturing that perfect moment is just the beginning of the art of photography. That perfect photo may be just that: A portrait capturing a childish grin or a peaceful landscape depicting a perfect sunset or moonrise. To me, it can become a watercolor painting or a graphic design. I see the structure of it and visualize it for what it can be—a screensaver, a graphic design, or photoArt. Sometimes the images I take remind me of the masters I've read about in Art History books, and I draw inspiration from that. It's all about the light some say.

To me, it is more than that. It is the merging of reality with digital graphic techniques that speaks to me. It may be the resurrection of old black and white films through the use of today's technology. Or it may be the art of interpreting a beautiful color scene into technically flawless black and white. Sometimes digital post-processing will reveal light or color or designs that nature hides from us. I love the surprise I find when I discover a new image from one that has been digitally remastered. It reminds me of the many hours I spent in the darkroom. I've never forgotten that feeling of anticipation as I watched my work appear after exposing and bathing my prints.

Photography has come a long way over the last 40 years. Today's cameras are capable of taking that perfect picture with hardly any intervention. And everyone with a cell phone is a budding photographer. Finding the *Art* in it is what intrigues me. For photographers today, it takes time and skill to create something unique. As a photo-artist, I am challenged with new ways of processing, new technology to learn, and new ways of creating art with my digital images. Some of my images are whimsical, some explore a particular aspect such as minimalism, and some are just representative of the world as I see it. This is a very new field and possibilities are endless. As the technology changes, hopefully, so do I.

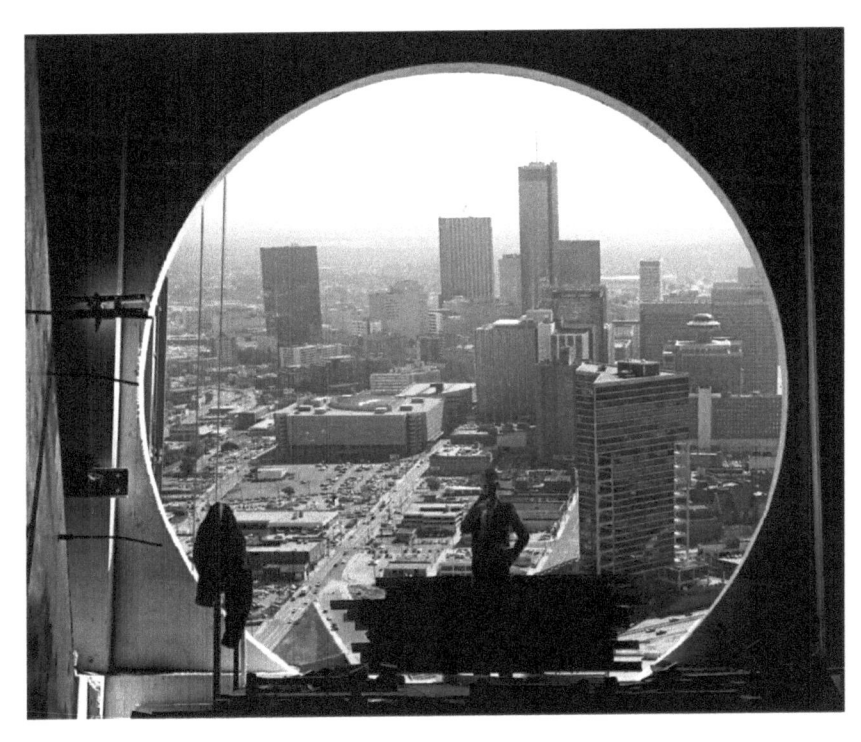

Uptown Girl-Downtown World 2015, Digital Composite from **TRI-X** *film (1982), 20x24*

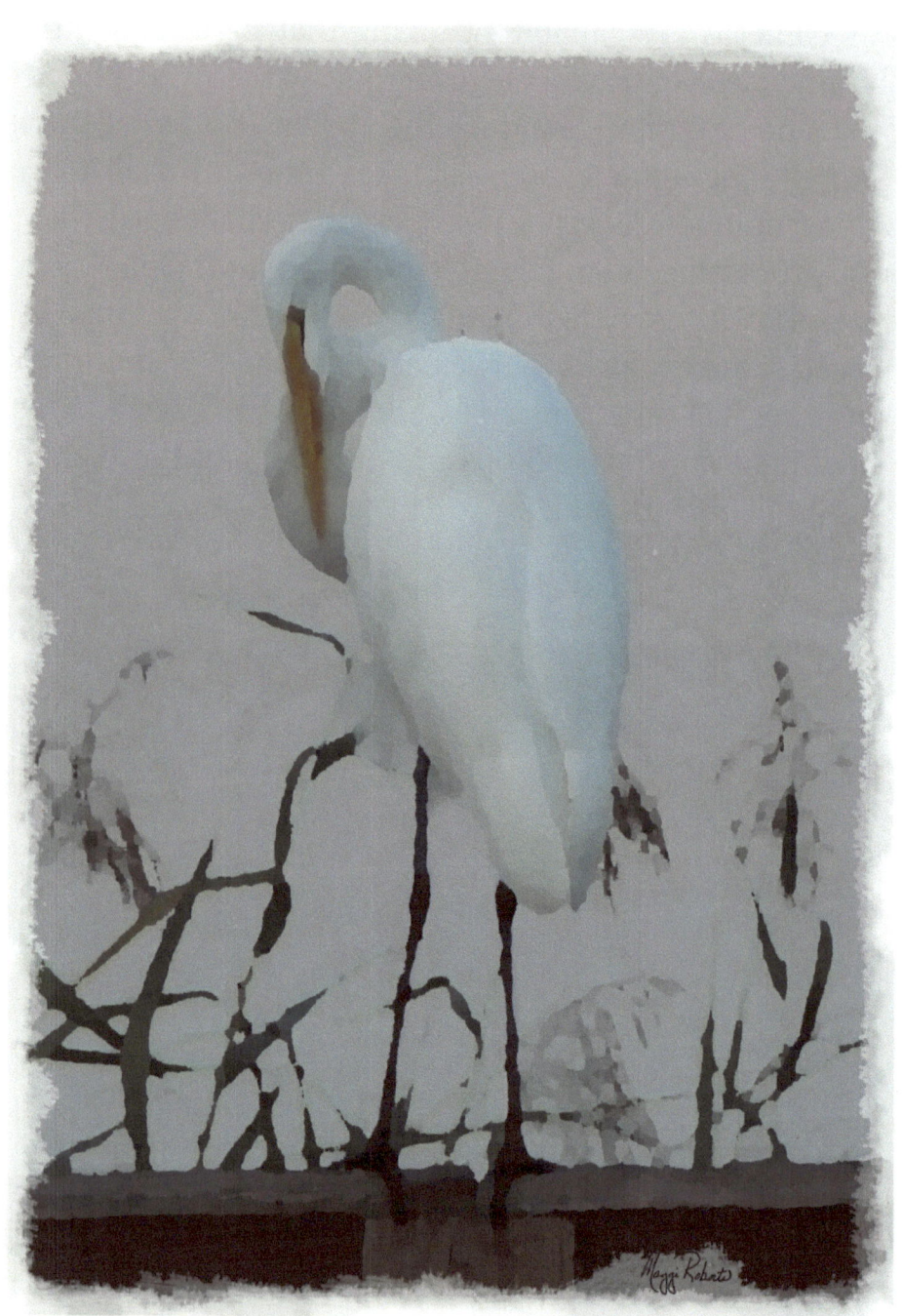

Great Egret, PhotoArt, 16x20

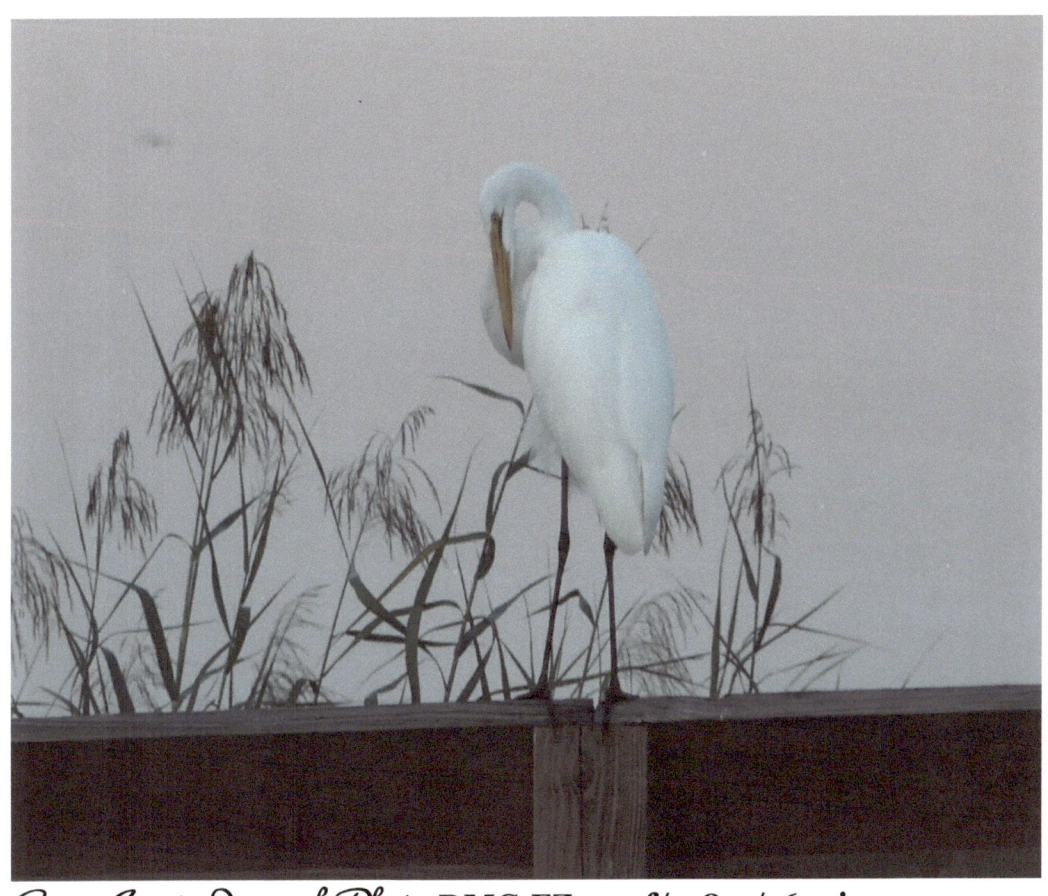

Great Egret, Original Photo DMC-FZ300 f/2.8 1/160 iso100

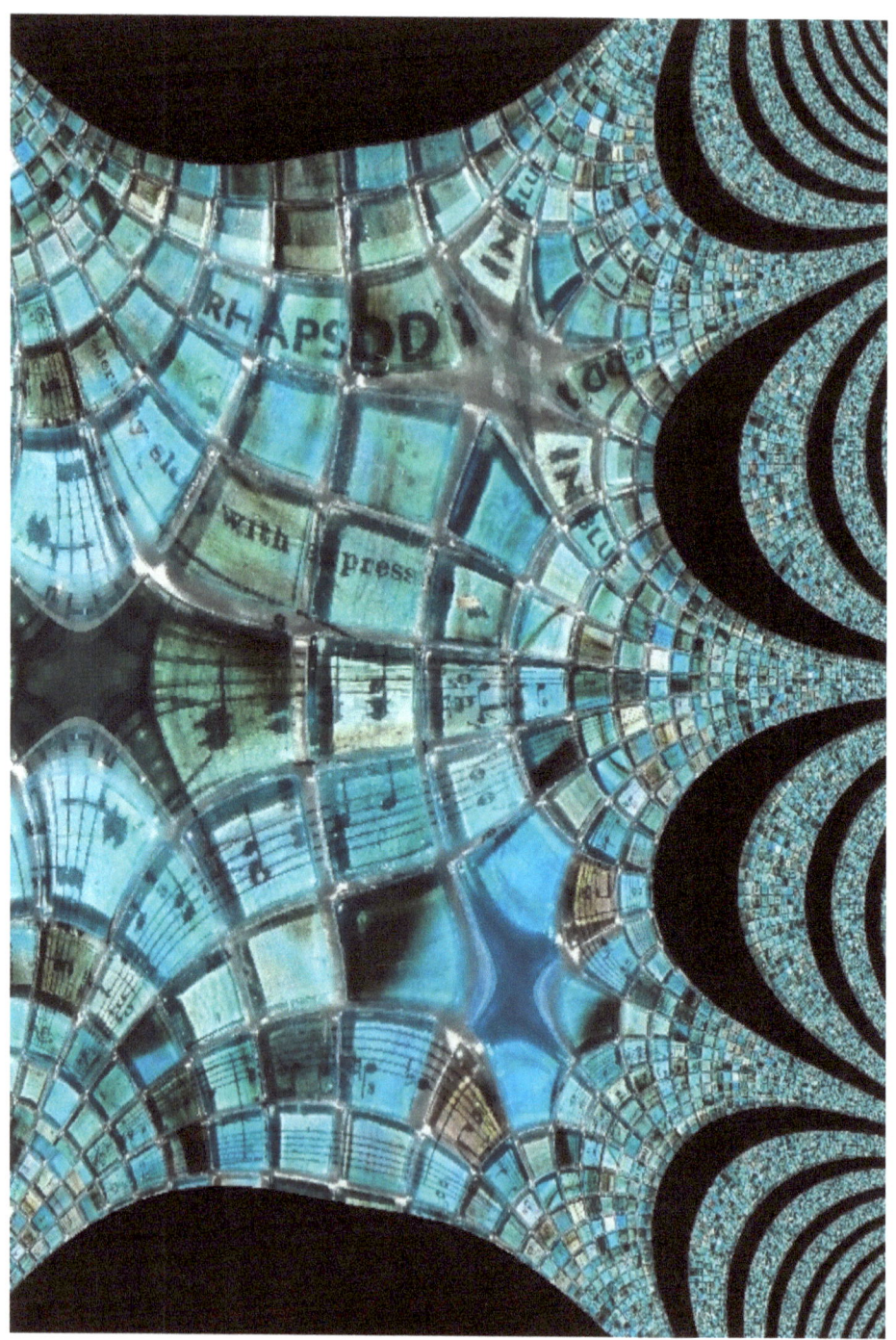

Rhapsody in Blue

MARA VIKSNINS, PRESIDENT
National Member

I am a mixed media artist who uses a great deal of texture to depict landscapes, the spirit of Mother Nature, and the sense of wonder in nature. Nature in art can take many visual forms, from photorealism to abstraction. Art can mimic nature by seeking to visually replicate objects as they actually appear in real life. But abstract paintings can also take their visual cue from actual forms in nature. In my work, I try to convey a sense of nature but elements are abstracted so the viewers can use their imagination to view the image from their own personal perspective.

I am deeply interested in the vast and rugged terrains of the world. The "striking barren land" Madre de Dios in Peru has been of particular importance in my work. Its name means "Mother of God." This name befits a wild, untamed wilderness, trackless swamps, and meandering rivers which are flanked by unforgiving terrain. It was believed that outsiders only survived in such a place by the grace of God.

This ruggedness reminds one of the Alaskan wilderness as well. Tundra comes from a Finnish word *tunturi*, which means "treeless heights."

I use mixed media to convey the loneliness and starkness to the viewer. The contrast between sky and land is immense, and I have tried to depict the intense ruggedness and utter loneliness that radiates from the tundra. Rugged surfaces are depicted by using textural elements such as sand, gravel, unusual media such as lace, handmade paper and textural found objects. I have recently explored using gold and silver leaf as well. I hope to show the viewer the beauty behind the starkness.

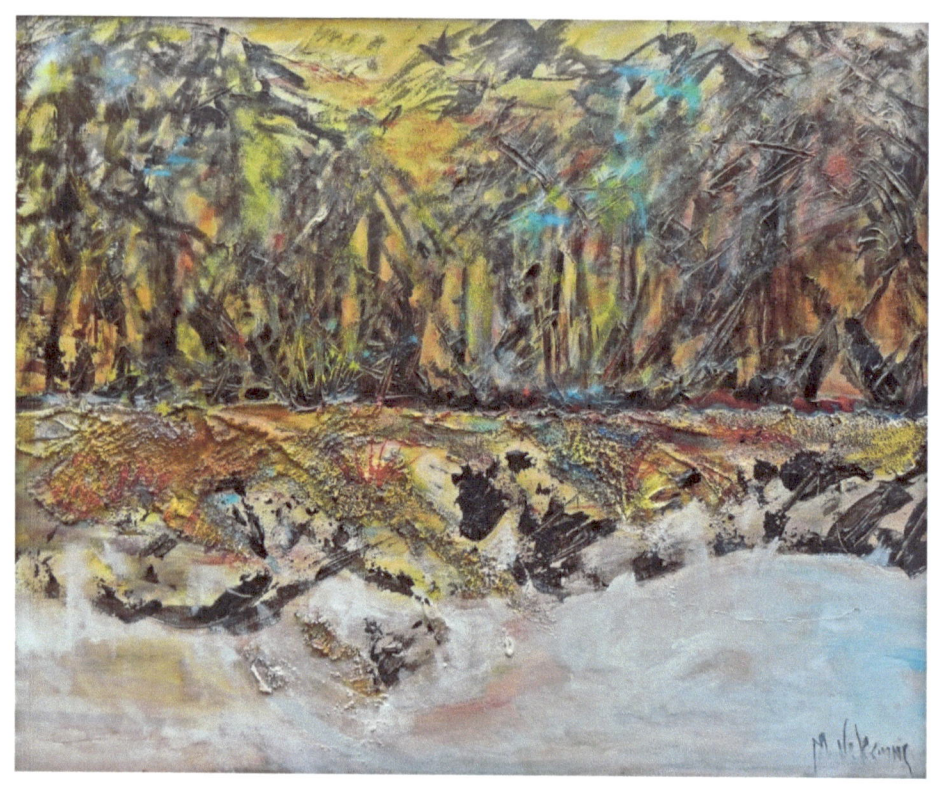

Windswept Shores

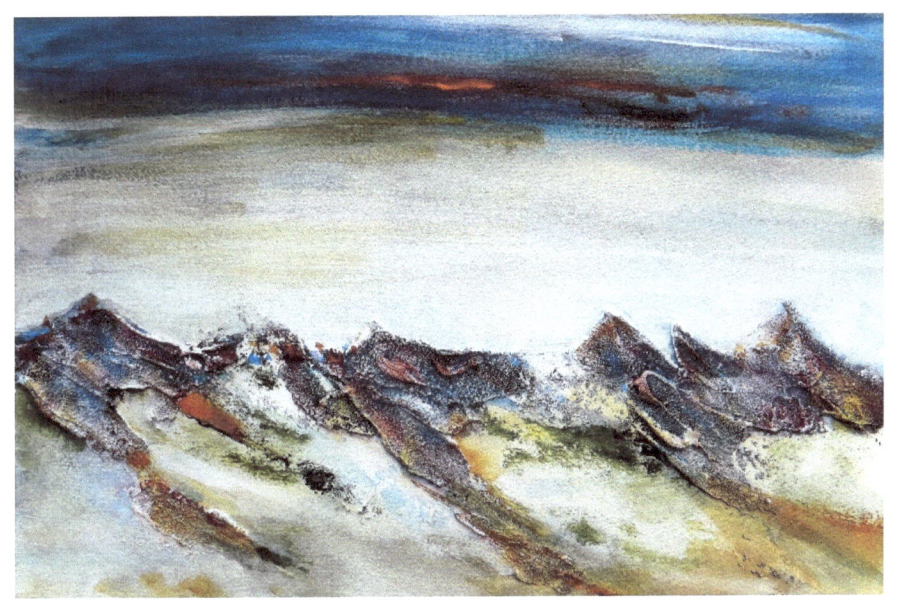

Madre de Dios

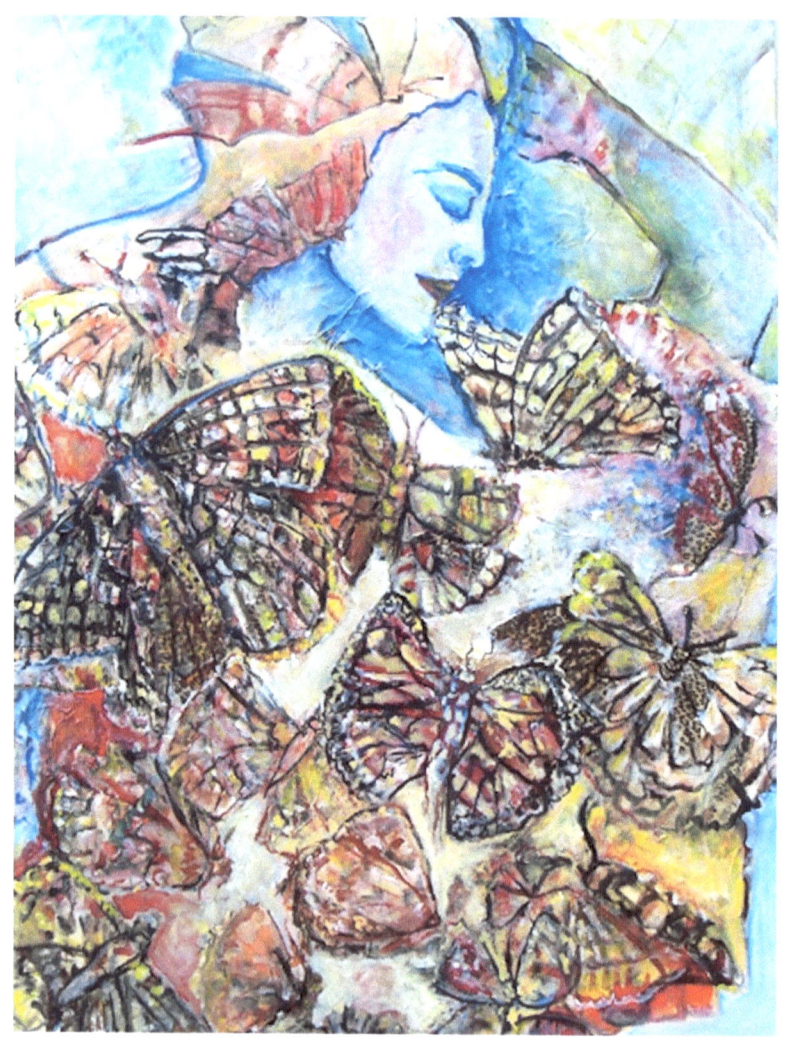

Fly Away

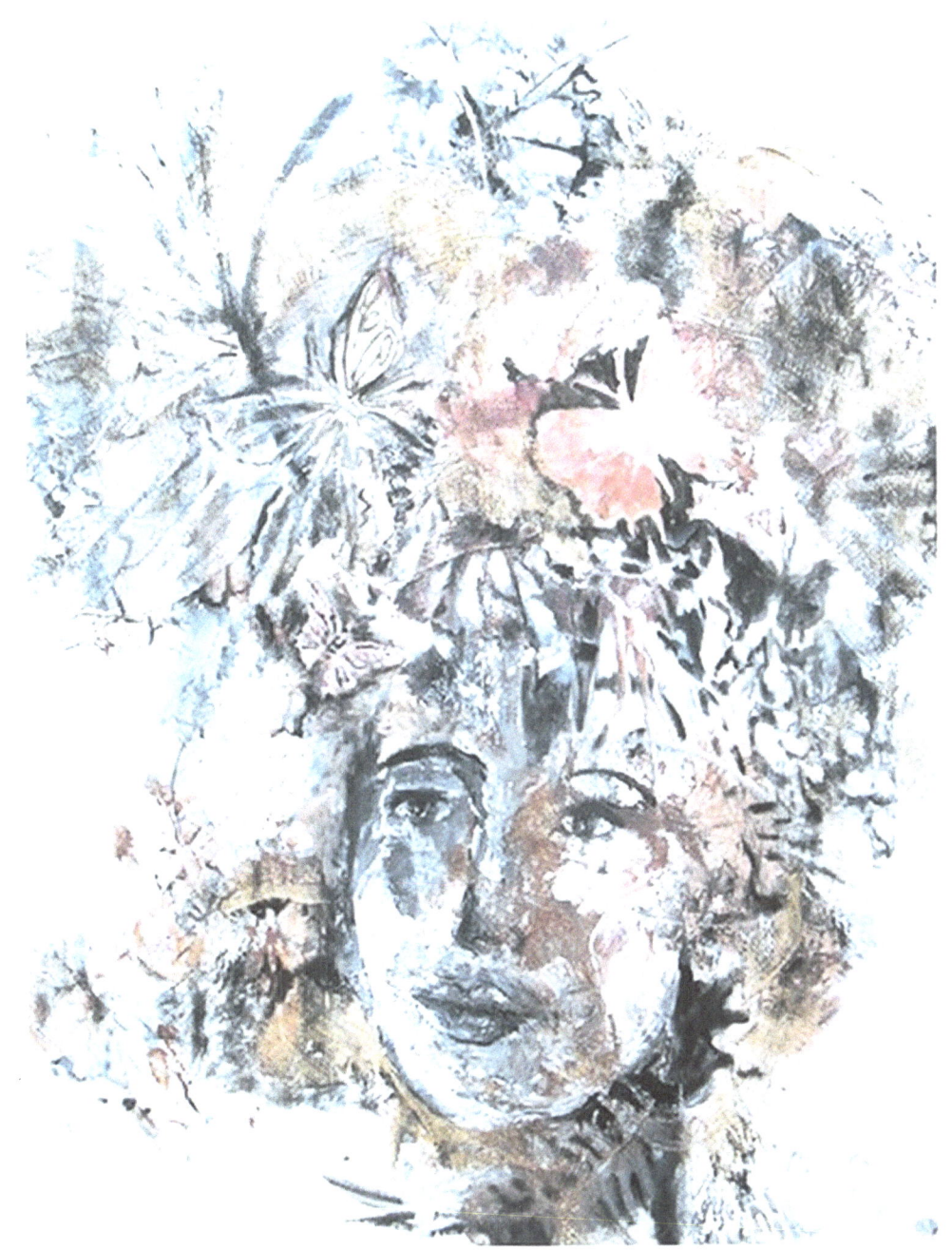

Out of the Woods

CHRISTINE SALOMÉ
International Member

What I like to portray is the invisible, the energy, the emotion behind the subject or the movement of the matter if I choose abstract art.

Since 1992, I have worked with watercolor, pastel, oil, and pencil, but for the last three years I have been more focused on photography.

My source of inspiration comes from singing, listening to music, playing the guitar, dancing, meditating, observing the beauty of life, either in nature, wild life, still life, city life, or landscapes and most of all the communication between beings, and the spirituality.

Like Henri Cartier-Bresson, one of the most influential photographers of our time, used to say: *"Photographier: c'est dans un même instant et en une seule fraction de seconde reconnaître un fait et l'organisation rigoureuse de formes perçues visuellement qui expriment et signifient ce fait. C'est mettre sur la même ligne de mire la tête, l'oeil et le coeur. C'est une façon de vivre."* (To shoot, this is in a same moment and in a split second to recognize a fact and the rigorous organization of forms visually perceived that express and define this fact. It is to put on the same line of sight the head, the eye and the heart. It is a way of life.)

As for me, I share the same point of view and feel more than ever the urgency to bring hope and peace through my art, more life to our lives, inviting us to awaken our senses, to enjoy the present moment in the consciousness of the heart. My purpose is to try to do whatever I can to give the world the best of my being and leaving it a better place.

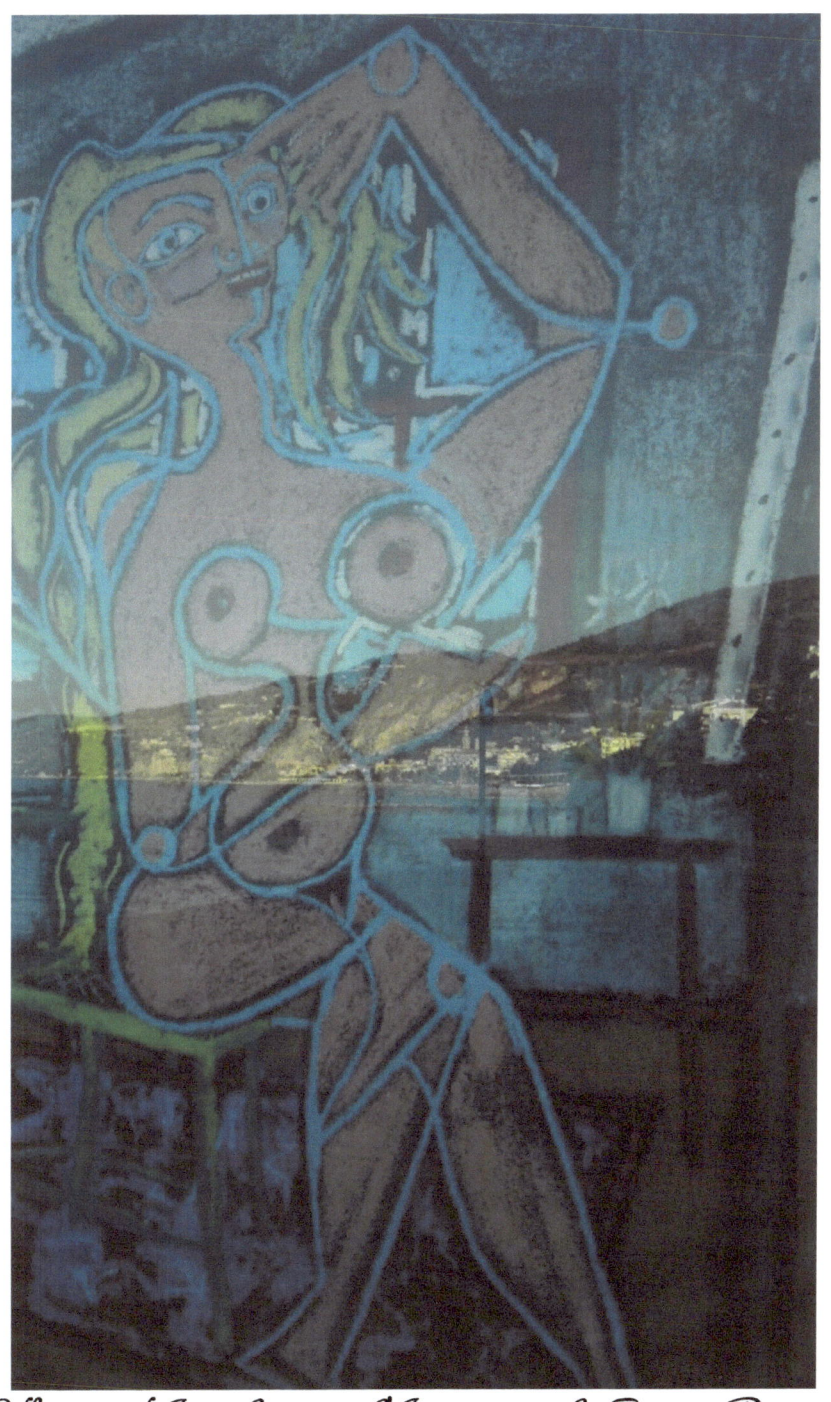

Reflection of Jean Cocteau-L'Inspiration La Femme Peintre,
1961 (Menton, France)

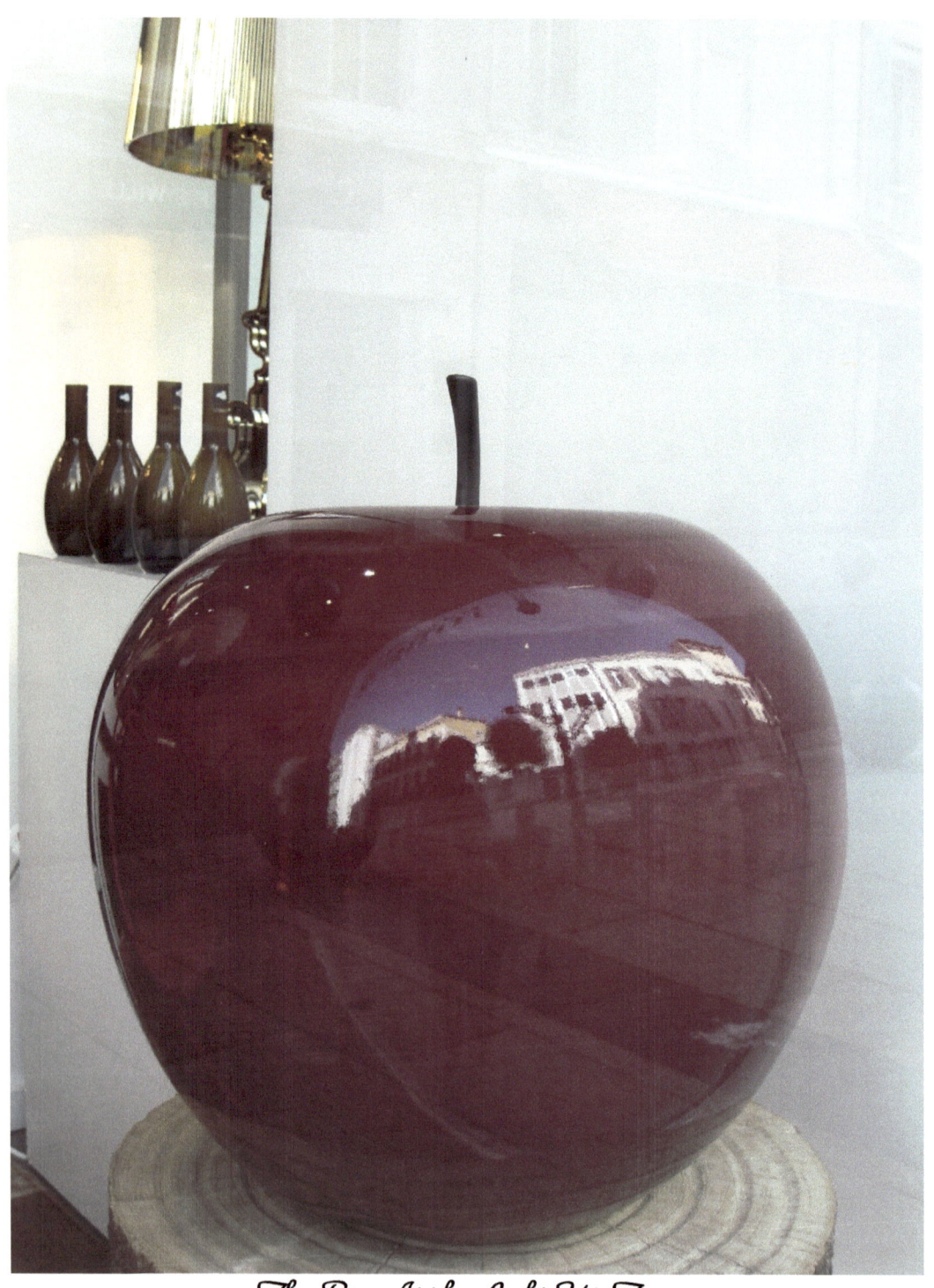

The Big Apple, Light Up Time

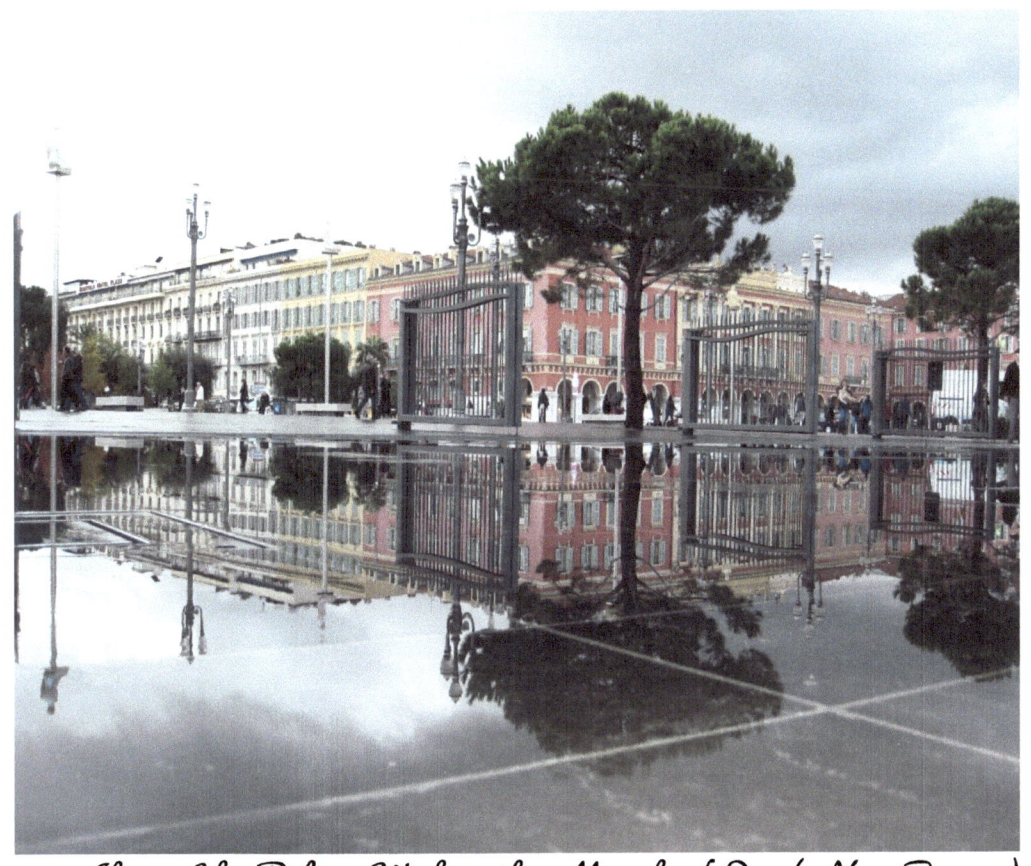

Above Like Below, Working the Miracle of One (Nice, France)

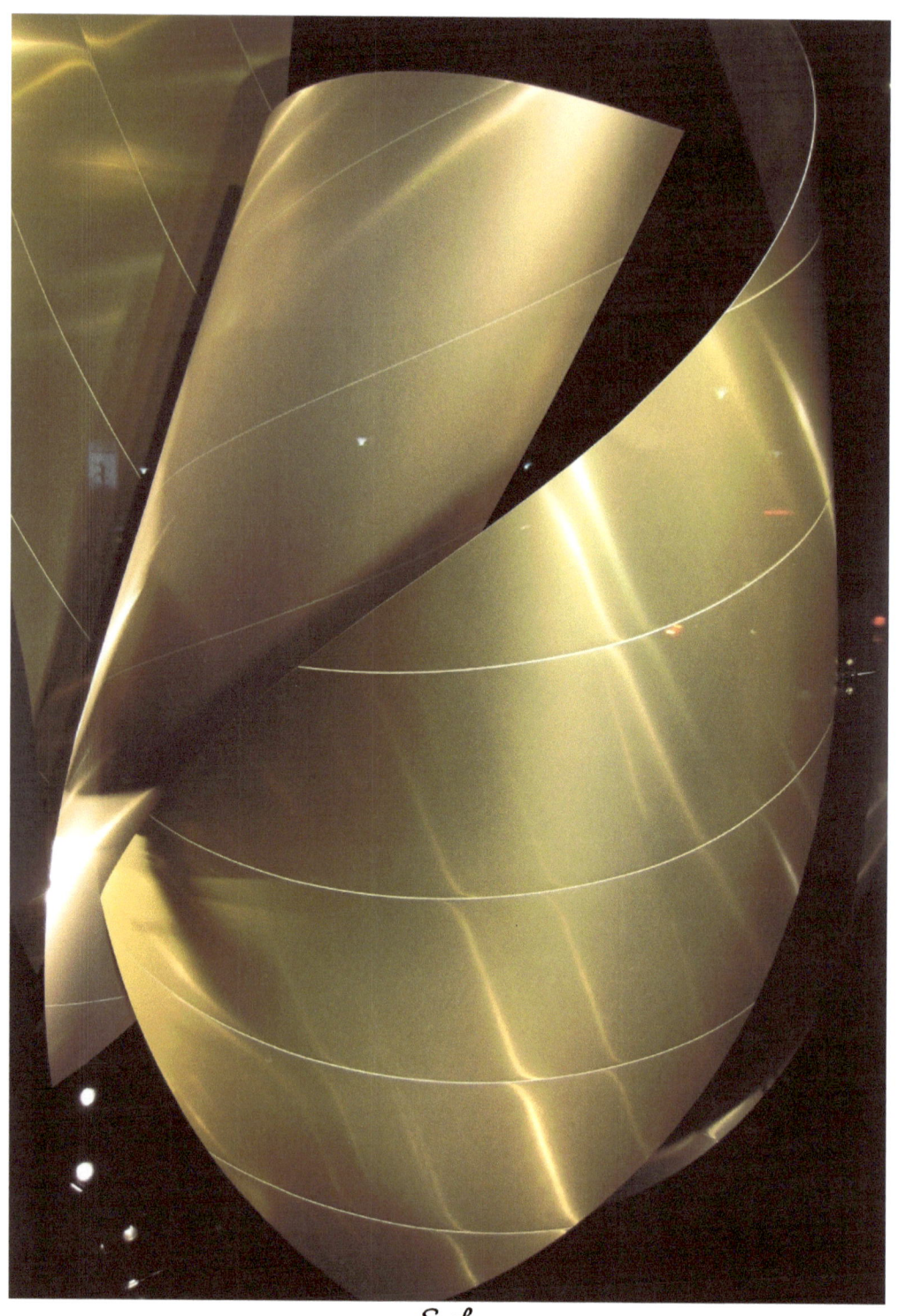

Sails
(Frank Gehry's sculpture)

ANN T. DAVIS

My appreciation for all forms of art has been evolving over decades. As a child I learned from my family how to identify colors, shapes, sizes, feelings, tastes, smells, letters, etc. But it was exposure to the elements of nature that clarified the magnitude and variety of colors, sounds, and sensations on this earth. As a young child I was literally mesmerized by the vastness of the deepest, darkest blue I had ever seen or could possibly imagine. Crossing the Pacific Ocean by ship for 11 days, no sight of land, just immense waves, the constantly changing shades of color in the sky, the cold spray and smell of salt water as it lapped upon the deck, provoked my awareness of the power, mystery, and beauty of nature.

From that point forward all aspects of life became fascinating to me. So much to learn, see, and experience. One lifetime began to seem like it would not be enough! In 2008, I overcame my apprehension and lack of confidence and made the decision to "attempt" to recreate an object of nature on canvas or paper. If nothing else, I thought, it would be a challenge. After a couple of instructions about paints and brushes, I began. To my amazement the process was relaxing and brought a sense of joy to my "spirit."

Beauty is truly in the eyes of the beholder, and while the pictures I paint may or may not be well thought of, they bring me pleasure. The mixing and blending of colors to resemble shades I've seen in the sunrise or sunset always brings the feeling of wonderment to me. Since joining my group of friends in Pen Women who share my pursuit of creativity, I feel validation as one who aspires to paint for no other reason than the appreciation and enjoyment of the gift of life.

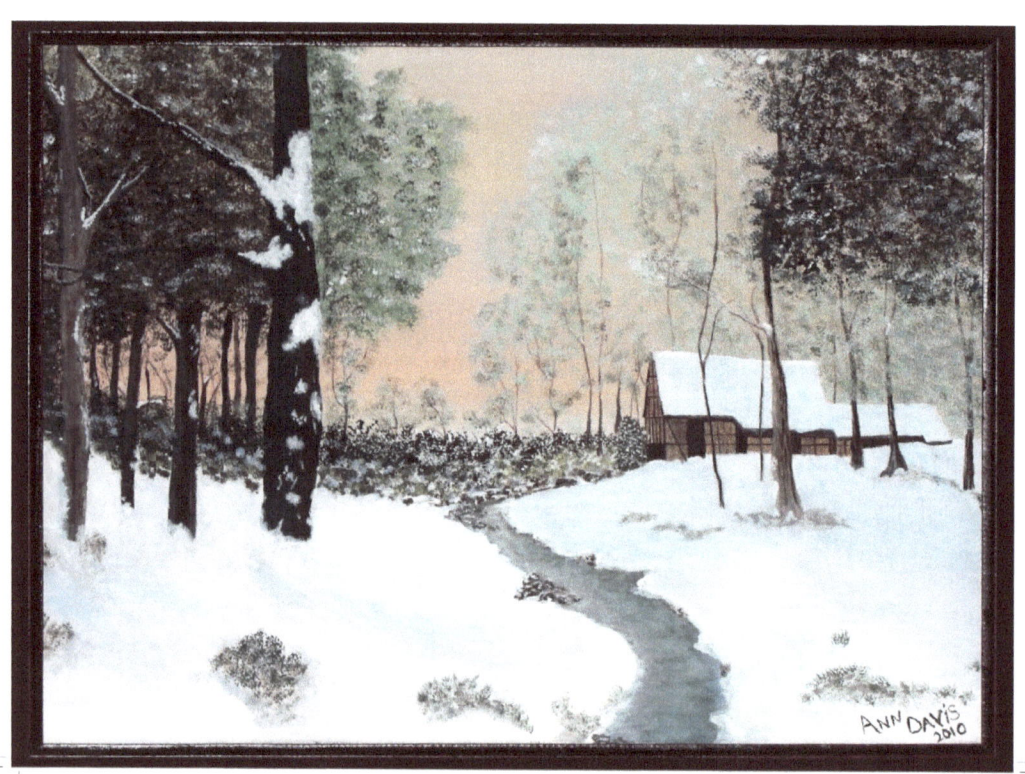

The Sun Also Rises

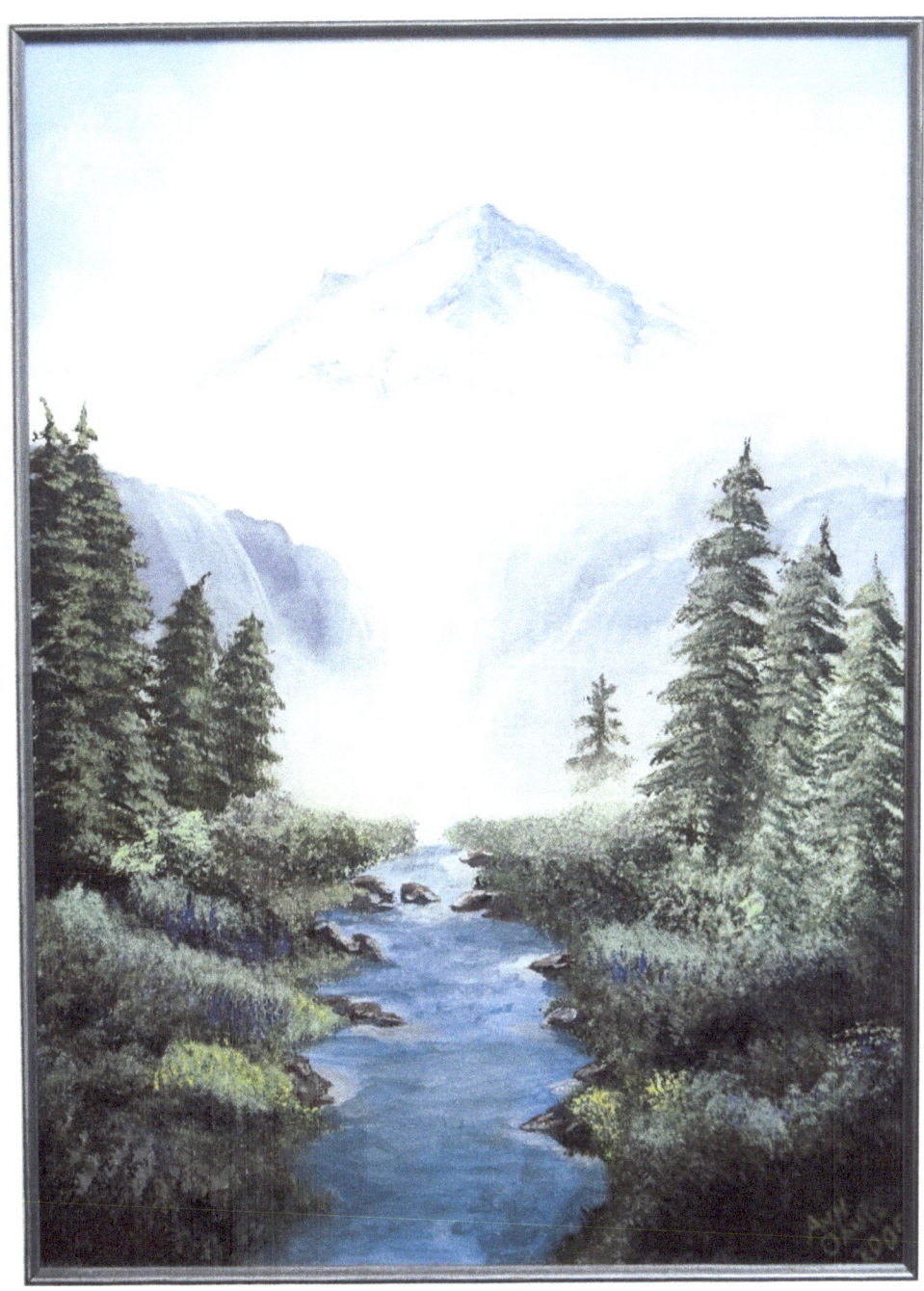

Tranquility

NANCY NESVIK, FACEBOOK AND TECHNICAL COORDINATOR
National Member

Whether I'm holding a pencil, paintbrush, or camera, chances are I'm really enjoying myself. For me, art has more to do with being lost in the moment than with the finished product. My favorite subjects tend to be inspired by everyday objects or nature itself: colors, textures, light, and shadows at certain times of day. I express myself with different styles depending on the medium, my favorites being acrylics and watercolor. My references usually come from my own photographs, as was the case with my snapshot of the little abandoned house in the field, which waited 40 years before it made it onto canvas.

I painted "Little Abandoned House on the Prairie" in 2015 from a photo I took of an Ozark Mountain's field in the 1970s just outside of Mansfield, Missouri. Laura Ingalls Wilder, the author known for the *Little House on the Prairie* children's fictional book series based on her pioneering childhood in the upper Midwest, actually spent much of her life in this southern Missouri town from 1896 until her death in 1957. The first of her "Little House" books was not published until she was age 65, which certainly encourages the creations still waiting to emerge from inside all of us! Less well known for her journalism, Ms. Wilder also penned a regular newspaper column for *The Missouri Ruralist,* giving timeless advice to women of her day.

"Life is often called a journey. Usually when referred to in these terms, it is also understood that it is a "weary pilgrimage." Why not call it a voyage of discovery and take it in the spirit of happy adventure?"

"... But the real things haven't changed. It is still best to be honest and truthful, to make the most of what we have, to be happy with simple pleasures, and to be cheerful and have courage when things go wrong."

"An opinion, supported by a good reason, kindly stated, should not offend."

--Laura Ingalls Wilder

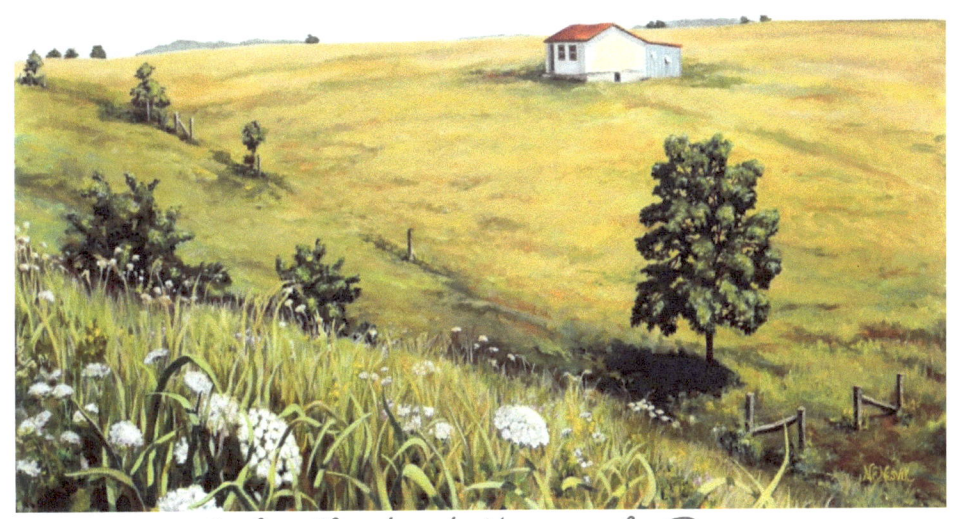

Little Abandoned House on the Prairie

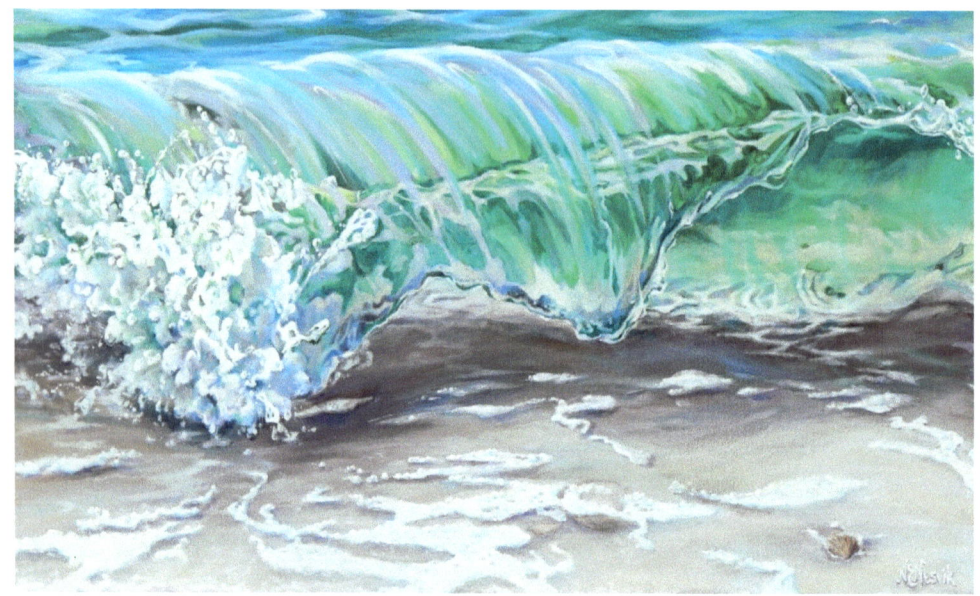

Wave

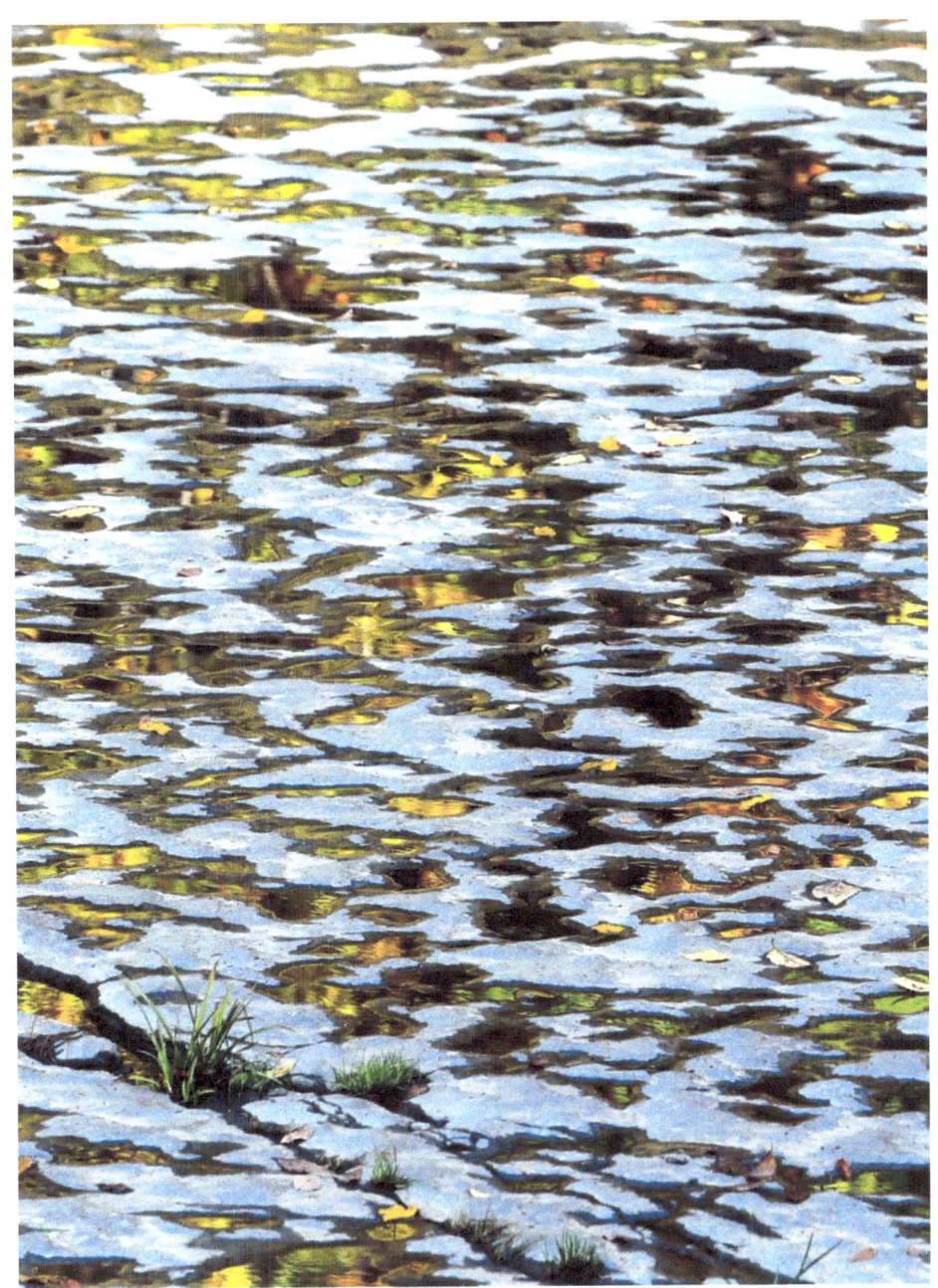

Puddles

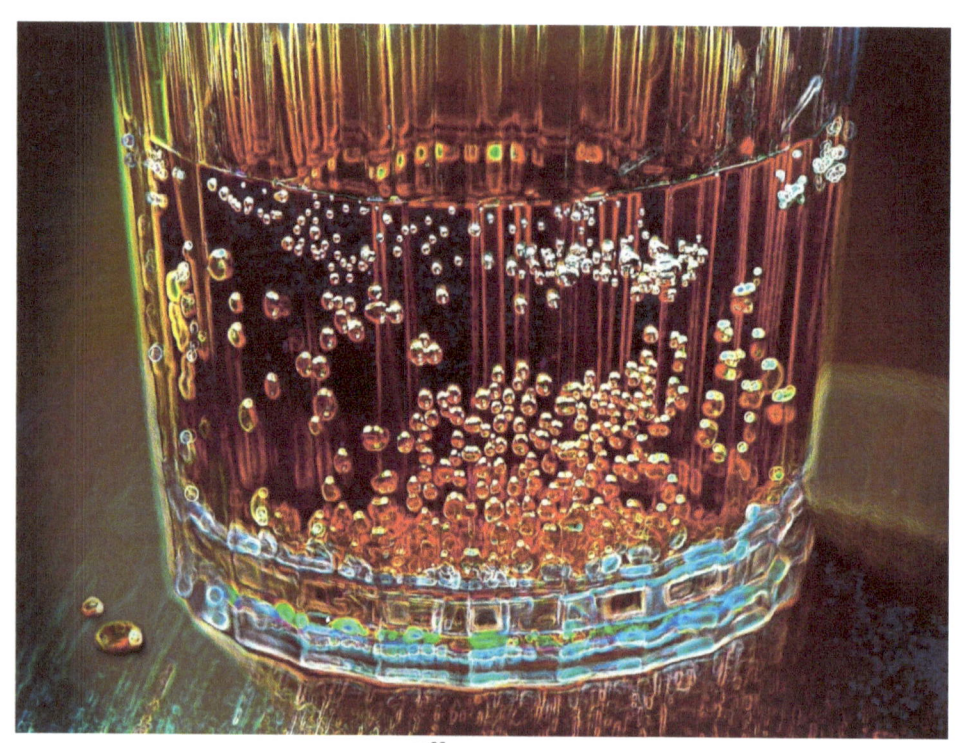

Effervescence

KATHY BREAZEALE
National Member

Growing up in West Texas and New Mexico, I thought nothing of being able to see the horizon lines in the distance on the long drives between our home and that of my grandparents on the Kansas plains. Not until I traveled to places that had forests and oceans and rivers and mountains did I realize the difference in topography first hand. Sunlight is different in New Mexico. The sky appears higher when your horizon line is 20 or 50 miles, and not interrupted by trees or buildings. Colors in Texas summers can appear scorched. Oh, but the wildflowers in the spring and the blue sky in the fall are spectacular. Outcroppings of rocks contain the history of the planet and petroglyphs from those who came before us. Those experiences led to my interest in geology, geography, maps, and the symbols early peoples created either to prove they existed, or to leave markers for future travelers.

To me, the beauty of the visual art of abstracts is that the viewer is not told what to see. One might get a glimpse of what the artist envisions, but the subjects-lines-colors-textures can be interpreted uniquely through the lens of each person who experiences the art.

Painting with water media, I layer many colors of paint onto paper, then sand, scrape, and burnish through the numerous layers to find what appears from underneath. Each time, it is a surprise.

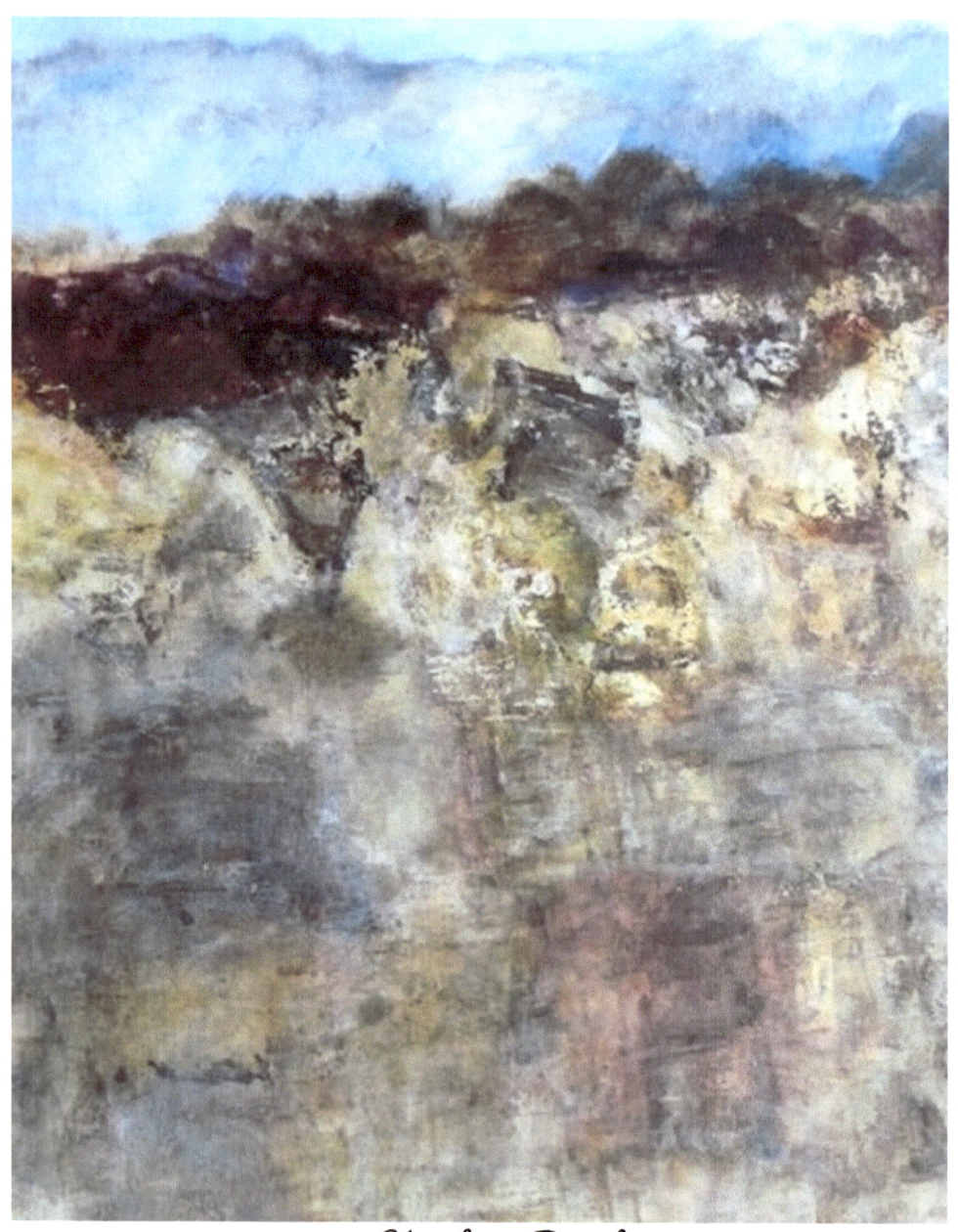

Vanishing Portals

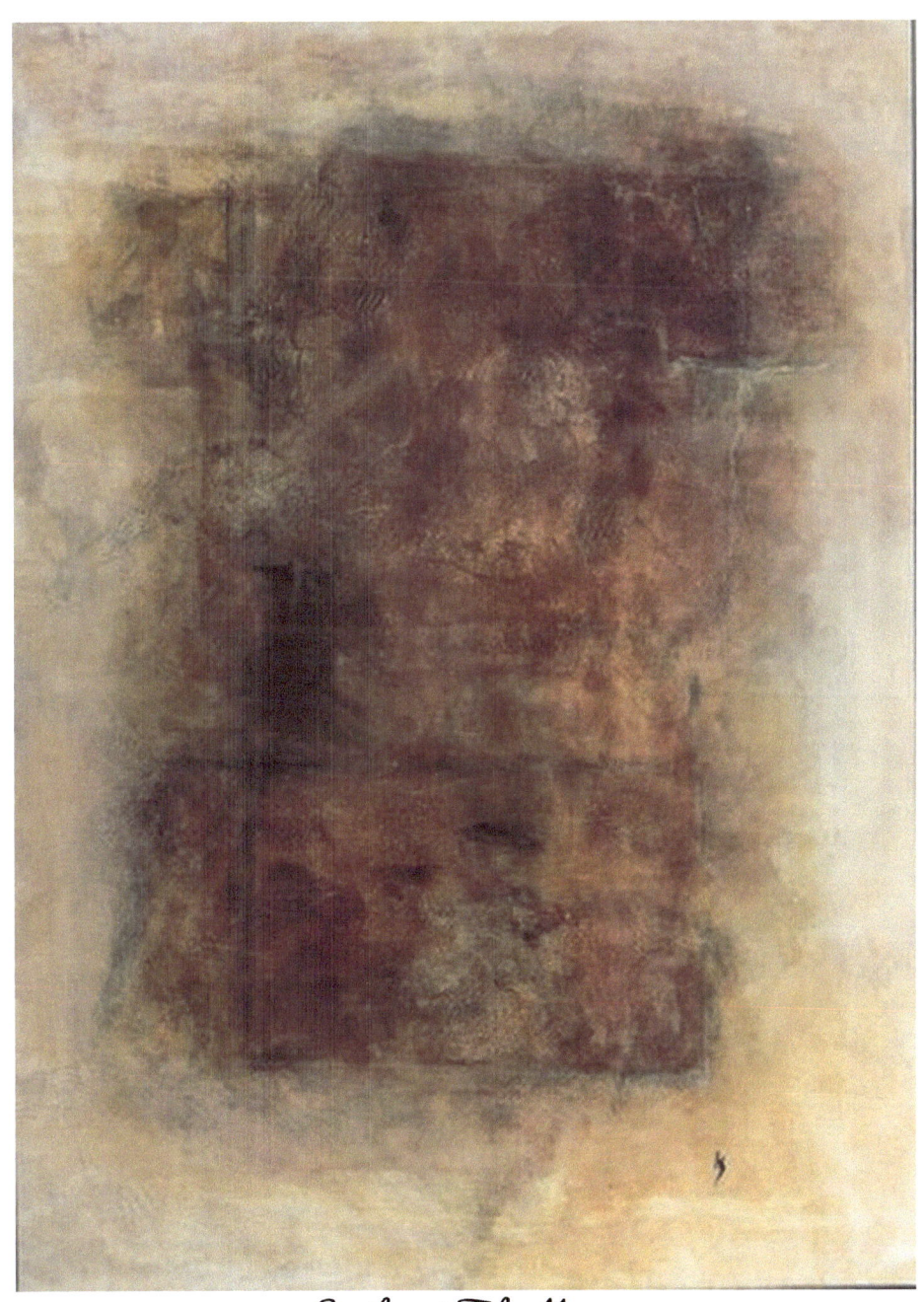

Southwest Til Morning

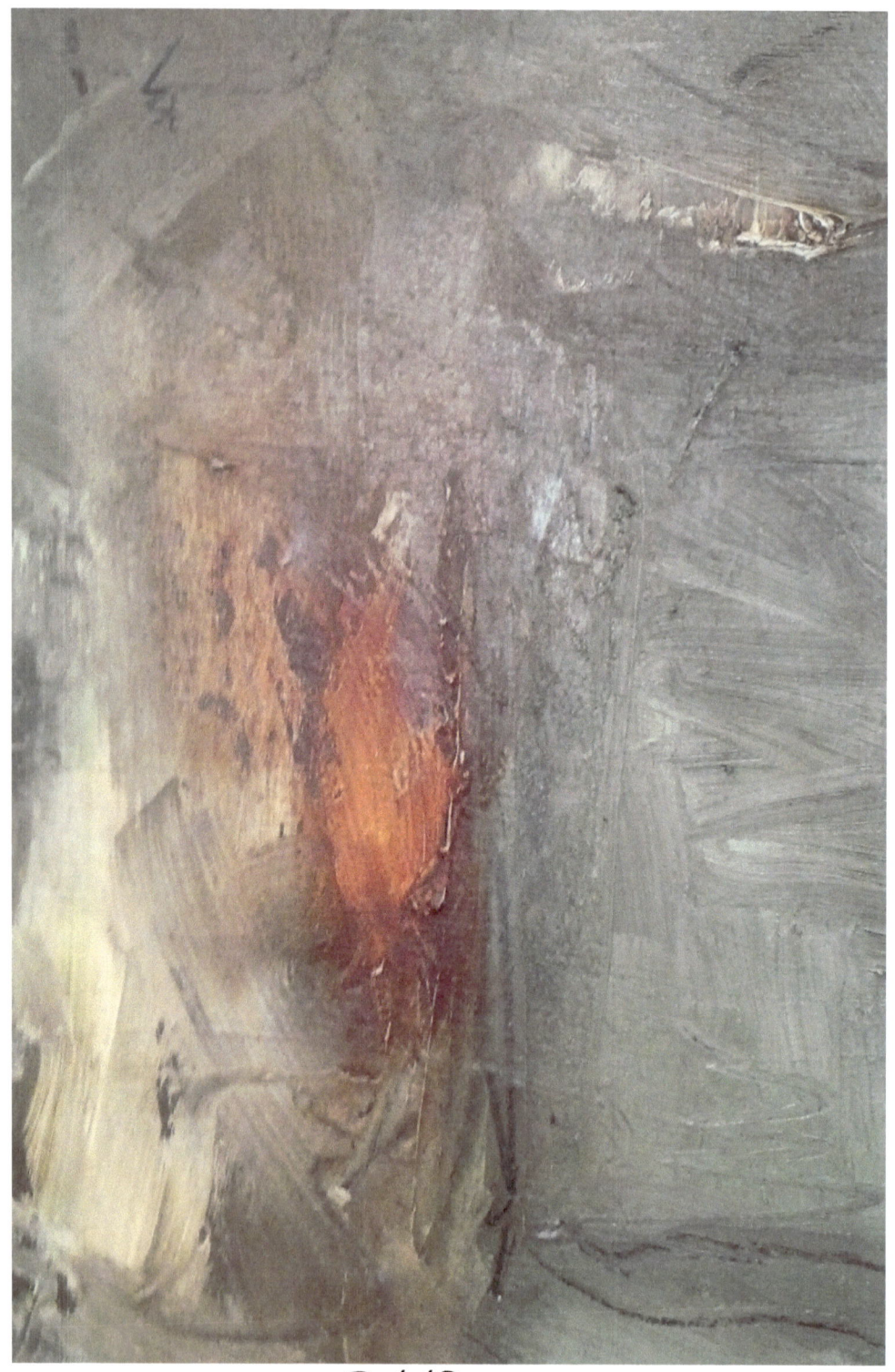

Faded Dance

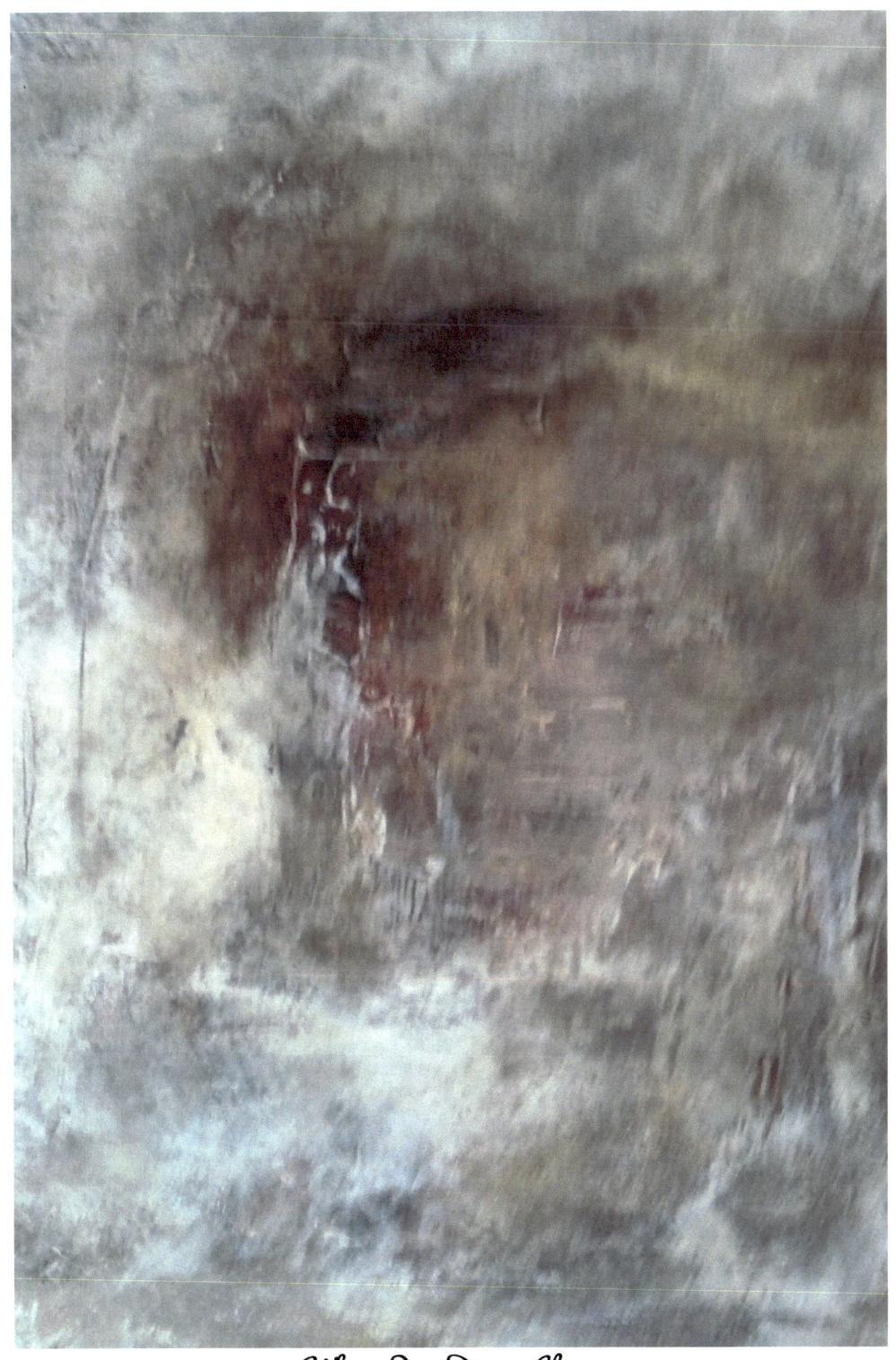

When One Door Closes

LINDA DEVINS

My body of work is varied and eclectic because almost every artistic endeavor is interesting to me in some way. I paint and love to do seascapes because I live near the shore. I construct from my own design dolls that are nationally recognized and have appeared in national doll magazines. And I have never met a bead I didn't like. But rather than just a straightforward stringing, I like constructing complicated and very large designs because they seem to be the kind of thing I like to wear. I have a wonderful family that supports my work and without them I would feel incomplete.

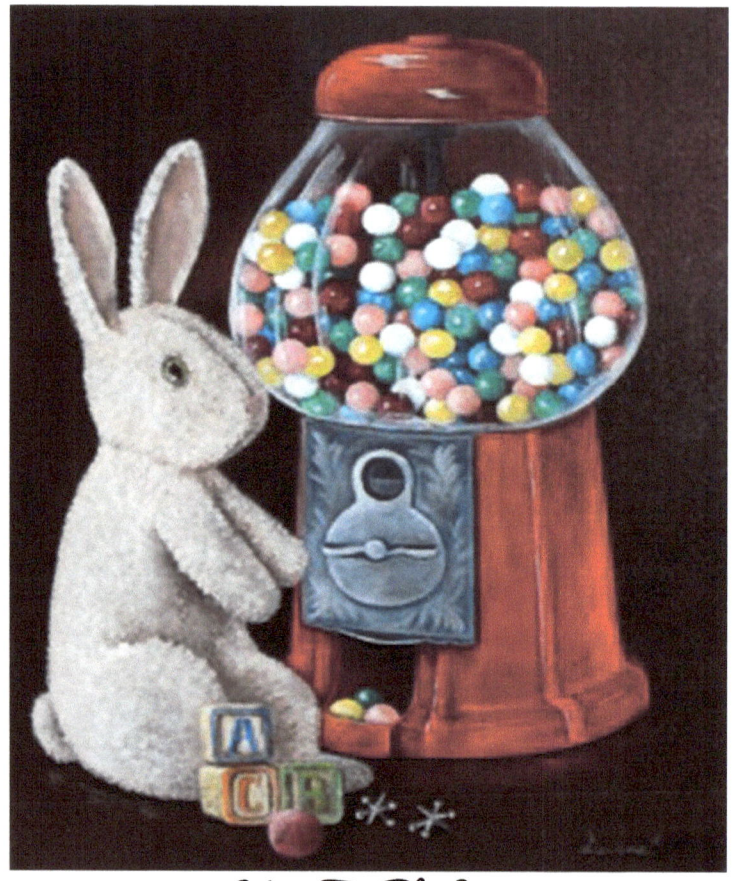

Want To Play?

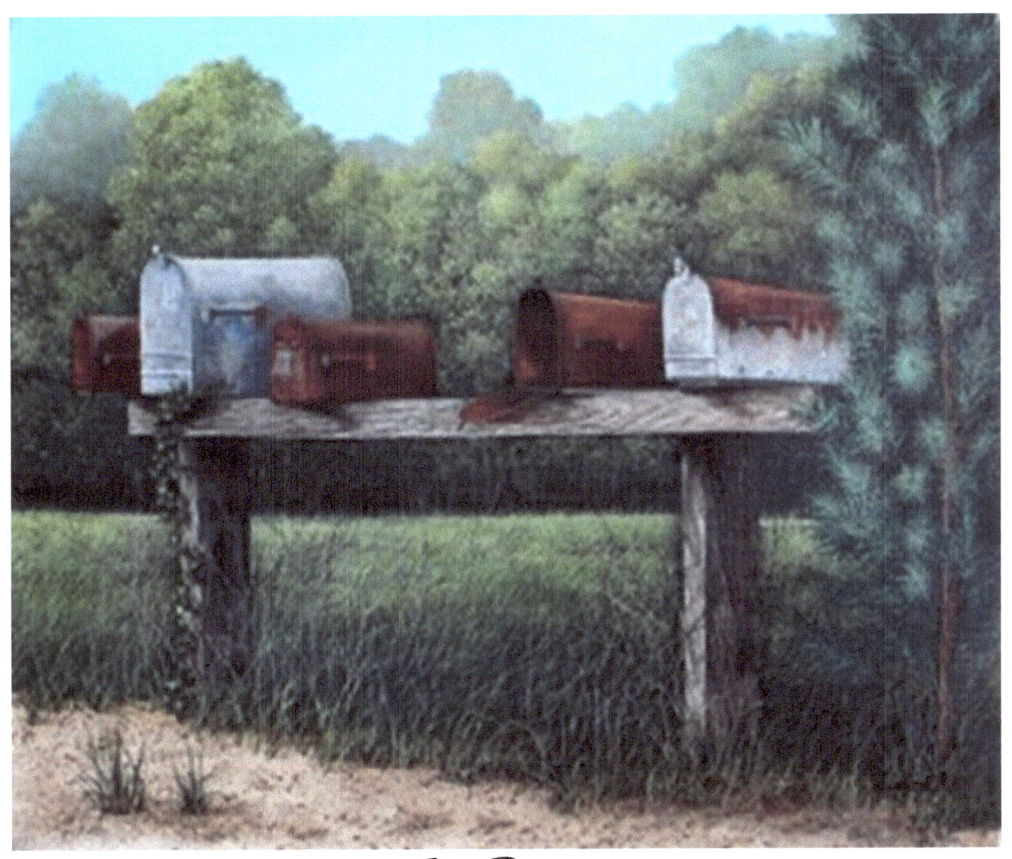

East Brewton

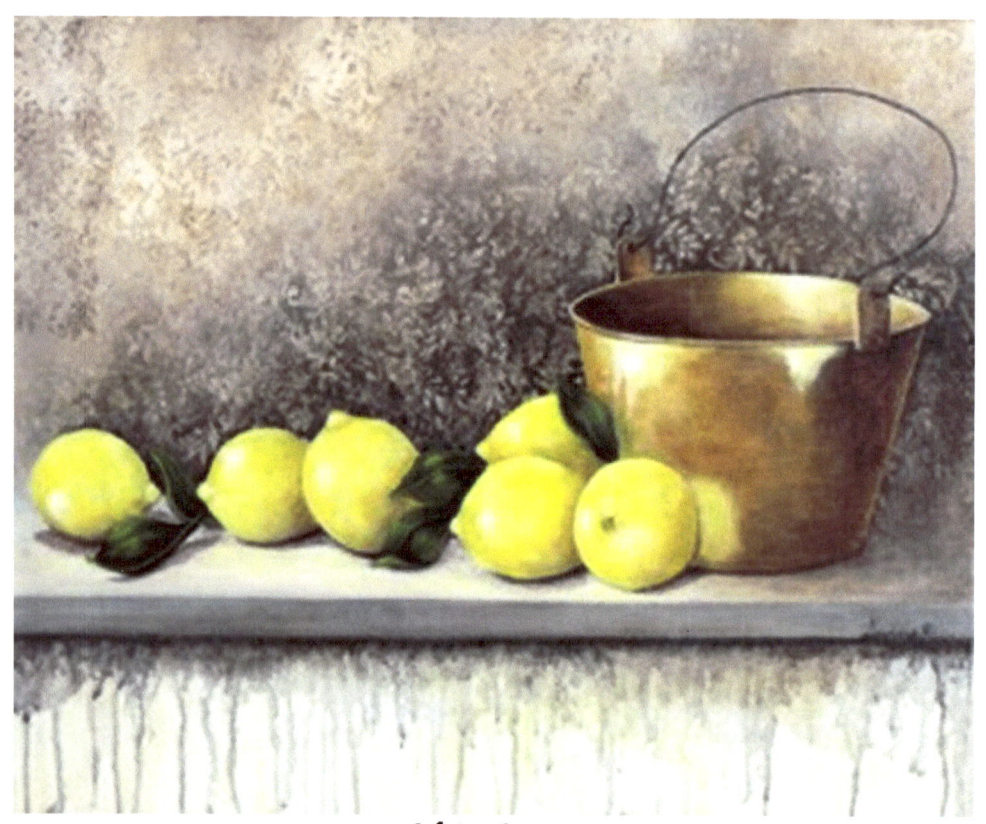

Life's Lemons

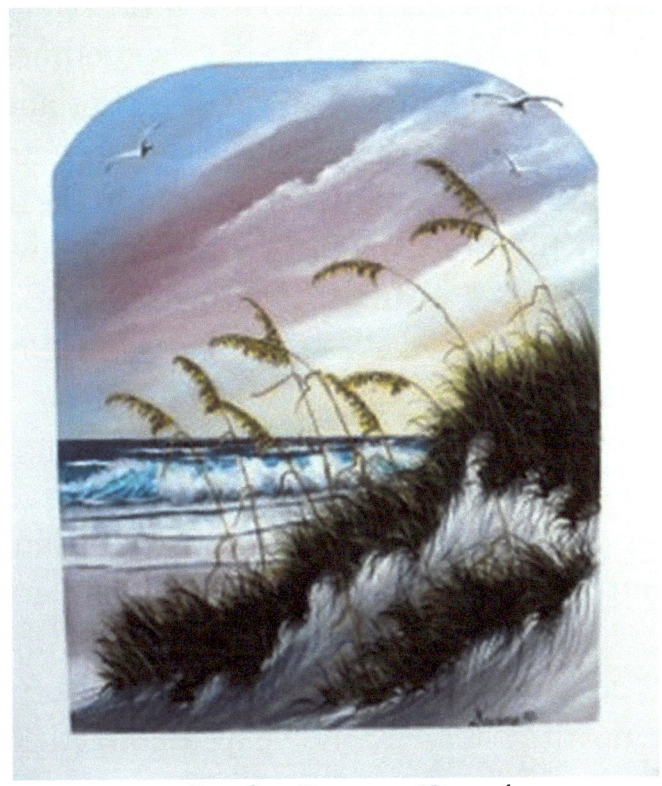

Another Day in Paradise

KAREN MCAFERTY MORRIS

I get lots of my inspiration while sitting on my back porch.

There is the bayou channel, like a little river--sometimes still, sometimes flowing out to the bay, sometimes reversing, pushed to its source by the tides, abode of turtles and ducks and mullet, and, in winter, brown pelicans that gather on low sandbanks in great numbers to rest and warm in the sun.

There are the birds. Cardinals, jays, woodpeckers, sparrows, blackbirds swoop and flit and perch, sending out their infinite variety of sound waves like invisible contrails, tiny airplanes that they are. Mockingbirds are the divas—you can sit for 20 minutes as they practice their repertoires, and never hear a song repeated.

There are the trees. Longleaf pines, live oak, laurel, cypress, river birch, and the popcorn tree (an invasive species that has conquered my heart because its changing leaves are just about the only fall color we get here in the Florida panhandle). Squirrels run up their trunks and leap among their branches, storms thrash them into frenzies, and cicadas pulse stridently from their depth on summer mornings.

There are the skies. Sunsets melt across them in hues of summer fruit (mango, tangerine, papaya, plum, peach, apricot, watermelon, cantaloupe), thunderheads menace and lower and simmer, the changeable moon-shapes arc across them, ospreys and hawks chase their prey, clouds shape-shift—from animals to cursive script. The Blue Angels, practicing on Tuesdays when they're home, shear them with their turbulent martial thrust.

Nature compels response. We draw contrasts between flowers' ability to die and grow again (unlike us), and comparisons (the seasons of our lives). Nature's soul-stirring beauty, its formidable power. Something—everything—in nature wields the power to lift poets' souls to create.

On my back porch I contemplate, ponder, wonder, question, compare, grieve. Sometimes answers come and poems are born.

But because, agreeing with John Donne and Charles Dickens respectively, "No man is an island," and My business [is] mankind," I see so clearly how lovely my life is, how lucky I have been to be able to enjoy nature and culture and friendship and family and freedom, while so many others have been so terribly unlucky. Thus, besides writing about nature, I also write about women, their vulnerability to fall prey to violence and hardship, living lives barely bearable, in cruelty, violence, poverty, and terror.

The three poems included here are about such things. "Aubade" (a poem-type about parting at morning, but this one has a twist), "Sonnet for the Women," and "Pantoum: for the Survivors" (with its lulling line repetition) all have sympathy for women at their heart. And the photo of the little girls—may they grow up to be happy and free.

At our Pen Women group meetings, we begin with poetry readings. I am always gratified to see how carefully the women listen and how enthusiastically they support my efforts. Occasionally, one will ask to have a copy of a poem, or drop me an email saying she really likes one, or how she always looks forward to hearing one, or tells me she gets mental pictures as I read.

Making this poet's heart sing.

Sonnet for the Women

So random where we are born, in what land
We first cry, a spin of the globe, a finger jabs down:
Excruciating sights we're unable to comprehend--
Buried neck-deep in an arid land ringed by a crowd,
Arranged for stoning, her tortured, slumped face
The center of arcane zealous rage and glee.
Thousands suffer in lives absent of grace,
Mutilated, beaten, sold—treated like human debris.
On my sun-bleached dock I smell the high bayou tide,
Sorry my sisters that you cannot know such a moment--
I wish you knew my grief for you who have cried
In some anguish you were helpless to prevent.
Can you forgive me when my fate is so kind,
When such valuing love I have for this life that is mine?

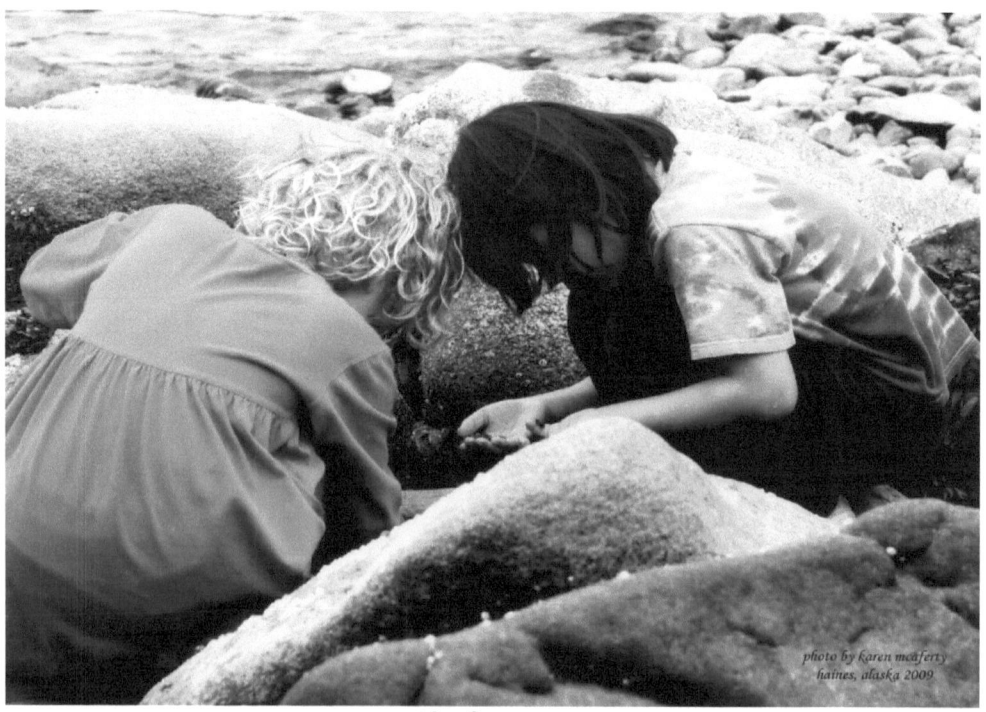

photo by karen mcafferty
haines, alaska 2009

Alaska Lasses

Aubade

How like an owl the mourning dove sounds
On this morning, as if they've been in a slow relay
And have passed the baton.

Waking up here, as the night-light plug-ins
Along the walls bow out one by one,
She hears the whispers of the cheap sheets as the other women
Shift on their narrow beds, their soft snores,
Someone's muffled weeping.

When she looks around, she does not see the sapphire blue
Lalique vase, swollen and faceted, demanding dance
From the light striking it, or the silver tea service
His mother gave them.

Everything, left behind.
Exchanged for this place.

She zigzags through the maze of beds
To the Pine-Sol clean bathroom.

The mirror is cruel but cold water
Soothes her tired eyes.
Her towel is stiff and clean
Like when her mother used to hang the wash
On the line, flapping like white flags of surrender.

She draws her sleeve down from her shoulder
To examine the bruise where he shoved her.
She presses a gentle hand on her sore belly
Where his fist crashed.

In the common room others
Begin to rise.
Each a phoenix in the morning fire.

Pantoum
For the Survivors

In nearly everlasting night the hidden cicadas
Grow underground, darkly unaware,
Long years later emerge to shriek in surging armadas
Staking claim to the trees, invading the air.

Growing underground, darkly unaware,
Moist seeds tremble, thrust and extend,
Staking claim as trees, invading the air,
Waging war with gravity and battling the wind.

Moist seeds tremble, thrust and extend,
We are born into brevity, and survival or sorrow,
Waging war with gravity and battling the wind
A panoply of victories and fears of tomorrow.

Born into brevity, survival and sorrow,
Some emerge to face cruel, surging armadas
A panoply of agonies and fears and sorrows
In nearly everlasting night wandering, helpless cicadas.

MARYLIN MCDONALD-DORSEY

Rivers, leaves, mountains, wind, sequoias and storms have colored my imagination and found their way into visual expression in my artwork. Translation of the natural world into form using stained glass, found organic materials, and the random calling of mixed media has been my choice for materials. Expression has been without rules, without convention and freely given to each material chosen to find its own voice to mirror my memories and imagination.

Each art piece has been mesmerizing to watch develop beneath my hands. Did my heart need to speak of forests today? Was my soul longing for the ocean salt marsh? Was my mind secretly feeling the birth of spring? I simply love giving full freedom to my work and expressing the handprint nature has laid on my spirit.

This exploration, this discovery of old memories of floating and drifting my old canoe on boundary waters, deep forest fireside contemplation, sleepless nights under stars gently amazes me. The natural world has always spoken to me, it has breathed out its soul, and I have willingly breathed it in.

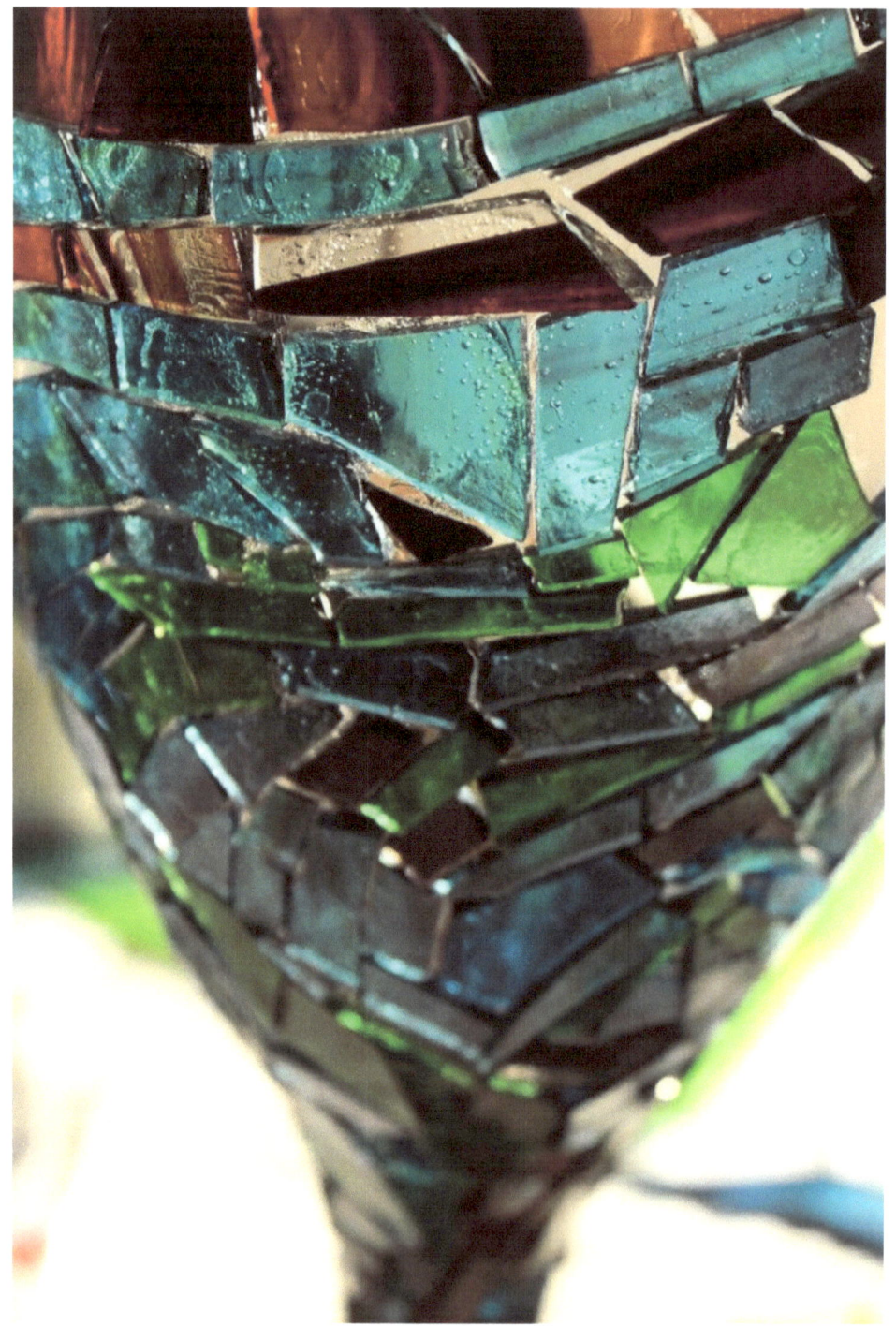

BP Oil Spill

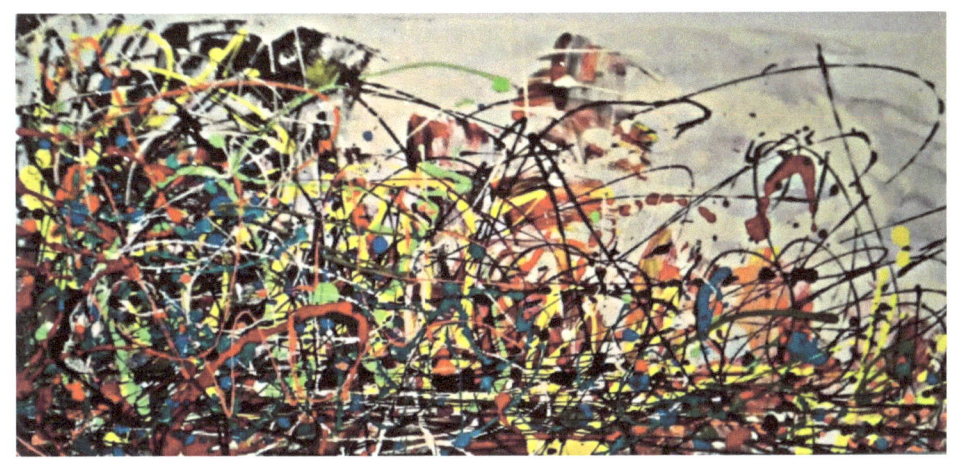

Celebration at Ellis Island

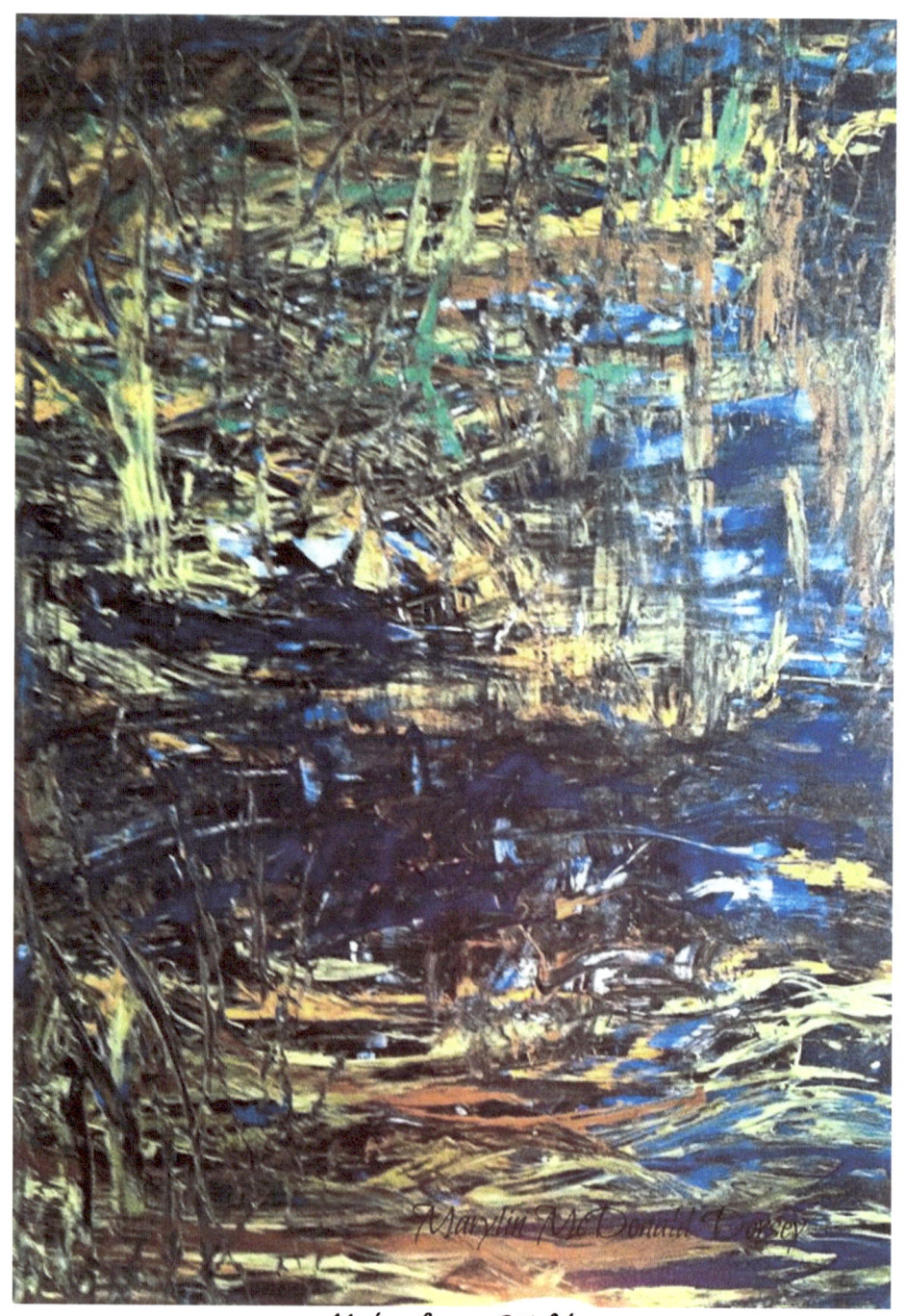

Midnight on Walden

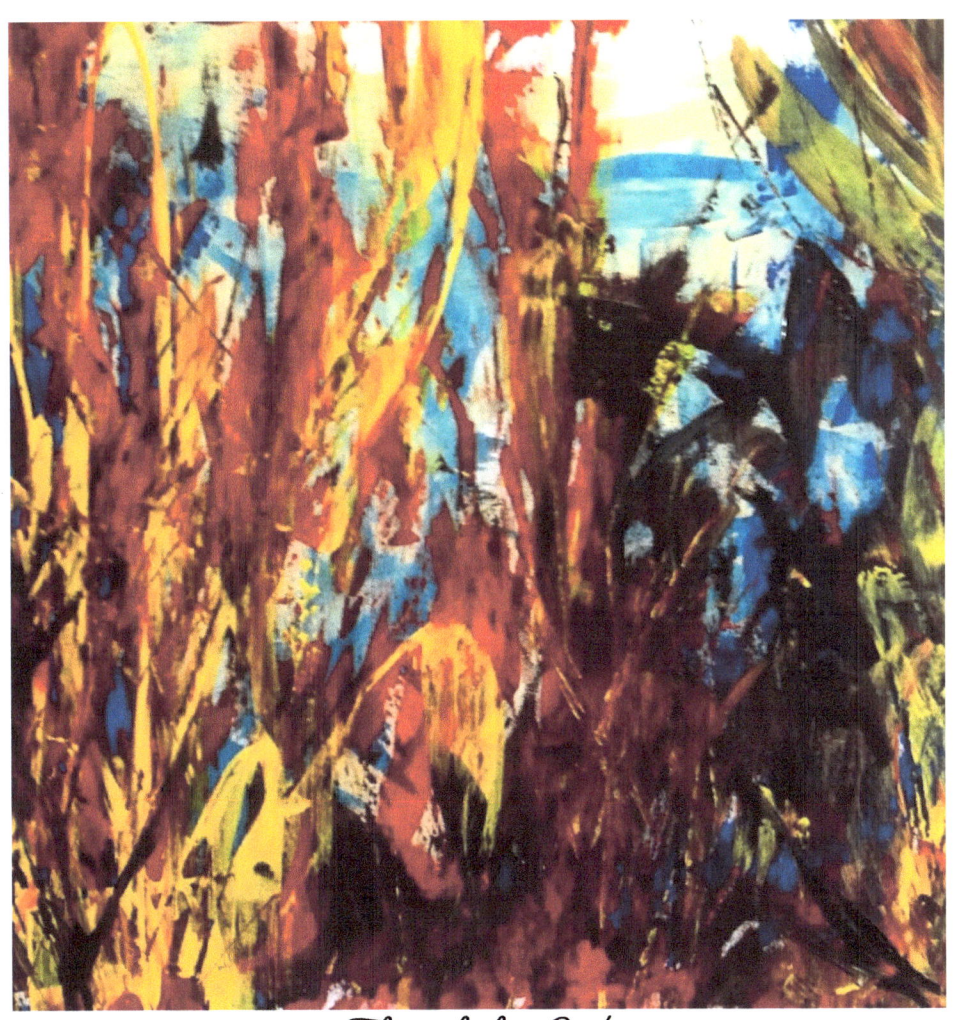

Through the Reeds

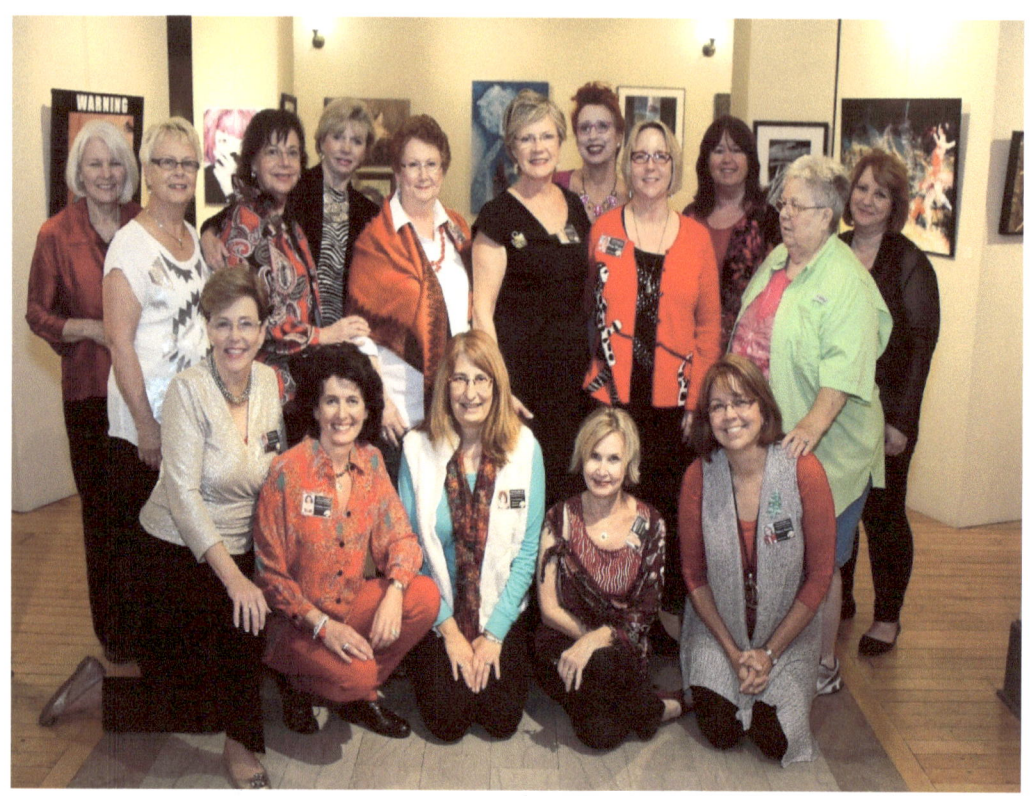

December 2015

DONA STENSTROM

Neugebaur's quotation "Seek out and treasure the sense of rhythm that is present whenever you write" was painfully true when I accomplished a piece of calligraphy called "A Poem Delivered to Friends at Dinner" by Angus Lordis in 1990. I had many teachers. Sheila Waters and Donald Jackson were at the forefront of my training as a calligrapher, and I was the teacher who inspired the beginning of the calligraphy club that still exists in Pensacola.

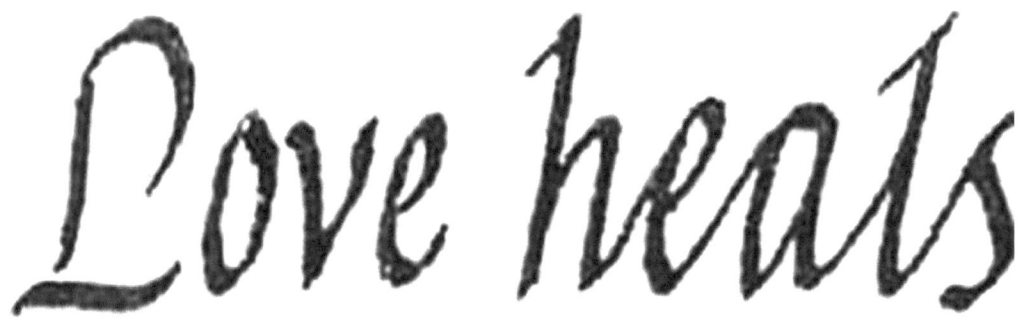

Phrase from "A Poem Delivered to Friends at Dinner"

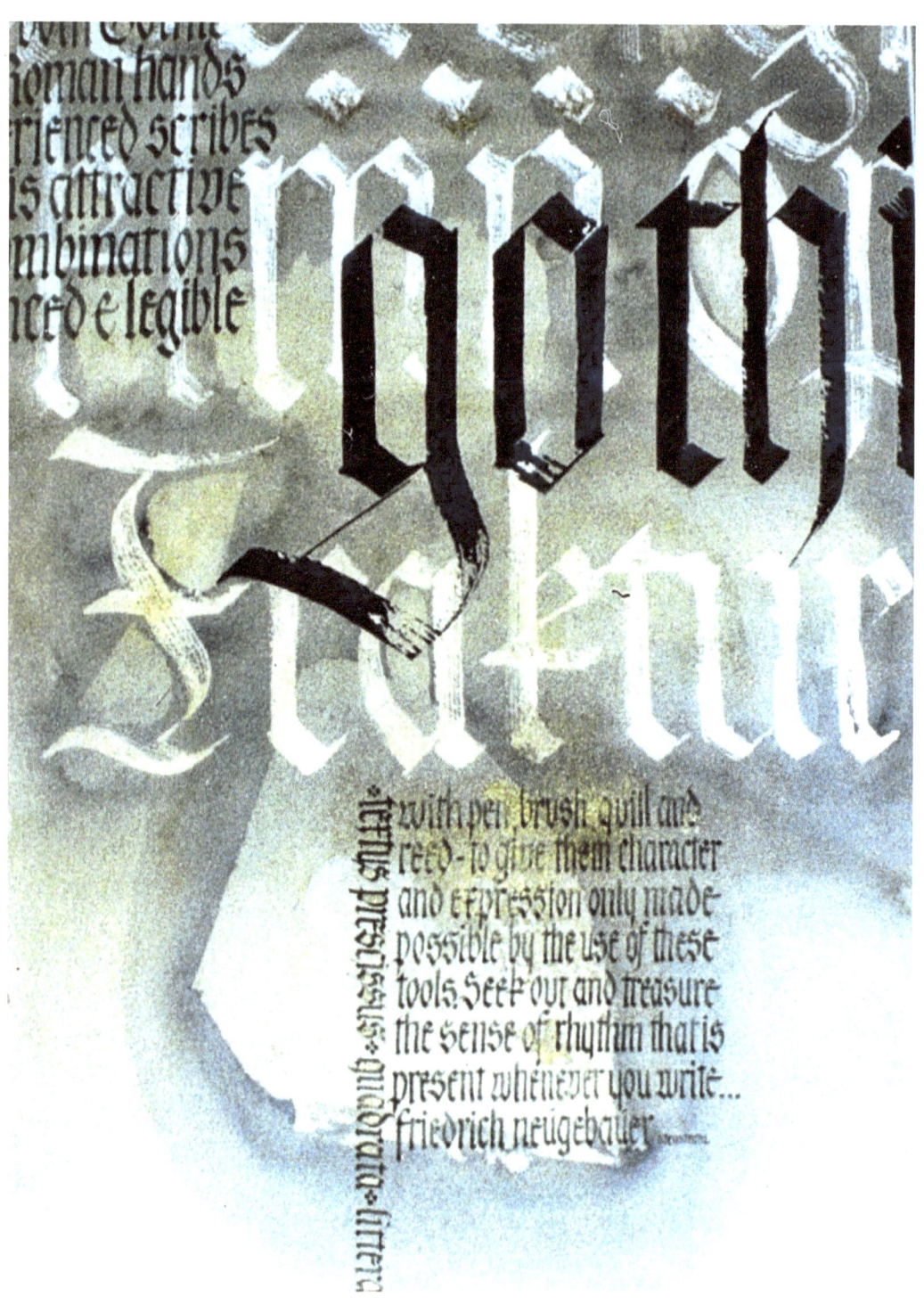

roman hands
rienced scribes
is attractive
mbinations
ncd e legible

gothi
Stature

...with pen, brush, quill and
reed - to give them character
and expression only made
possible by the use of these
tools. Seek out and treasure
the sense of rhythm that is
present whenever you write...
friedrich neugebauer

textus prescissus · quadrata · littera

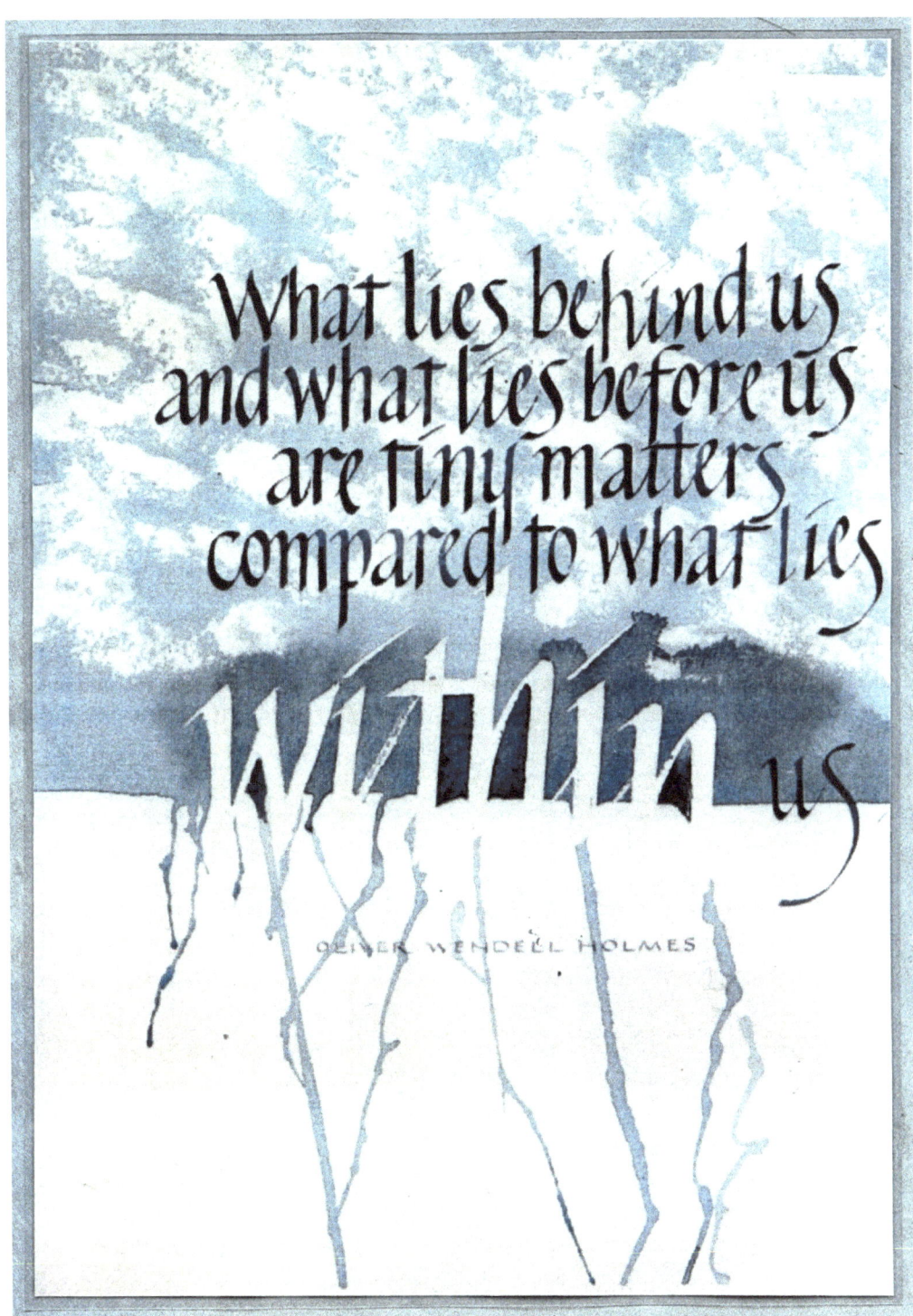

What lies behind us
and what lies before us
are tiny matters
compared to what lies

within us

OLIVER WENDELL HOLMES

AUTRY DYE, MEMBERSHIP CHAIR
National Member

I am a creative person. This attribute is visible in all aspects of my life. I create paintings and the written word that express what I feel, hear, or see. I take a phrase and turn it into a painting that expresses a particular thought in my non-objective and abstract work. Whenever I paint traditional paintings, I take the liberty of arranging trees, rocks, etc., that makes a picturesque scene. This takes place in order to express my response. There is usually a story or emotion I capture. My work is beautiful, thoughtful, emotional and uplifting. I am pleased when people think of my paintings as something they rediscover every day.

My favorite medium is acrylic paint. I like the viscosity and the way I can manipulate it to give me a thick texture or thin the paint to a simple wash. Acrylic paint manufacturing has come a long way in the last ten years, with paint that even mimics the movability of oils. If there is a need, it also gives me the option of repainting quickly.

When I have interpreted someone else's feelings, or captured a look in a painting, that is when I enjoy my work the most. This is particularly wonderful when you have been commissioned to do a painting. I am blessed that I have the ability to listen and help others. Not all people have the ability to express what they see or feel on paper or canvas. When I am successful, it gives me joy to help them realize their dreams.

When I can say a piece of artwork has turned out well, it means for me that there is a finished piece that I have brought to a successful conclusion. What it says to me is that vision, hard work and perseverance have paid off. Many times this is done over a long period.

If you look at all the paintings in my studio, you might come away thinking they were done by several people. When you see a body of my work, either traditional or non-objective, I think a pattern emerges, there is a commonality.

I love luscious color, some texture and perhaps text in my more contemporary paintings. What appears in my traditional work is enhanced objects or scenes. They have more value, deeper shadows, etc. I have been drawing and creating since I was a child.

My drawings were art. Sometimes I would draw not how things actually were, but how they could be at the end of my pencil or brush. If there was an art project in elementary or grade school, I was always called upon to do it. I was the child that could not resist a blank piece of paper no matter where it was. All my textbooks had drawings in the margins.

I can remember getting in trouble for drawing my fourth grade teacher. I don't think she thought it was flattering.

I think I identified as an artist at a very young age. It was not until I was an adult, and after I started selling my work, that I allowed myself to say "I am an artist." My connection to my work has always been a bit of escapism, and obsession. As I look back, being the middle child in a family of four siblings, art was the avenue that set me apart from the group. My family was not well off financially, my art supplies were meager. The basic set of colors was all they could afford. One day, not too long ago I realized I could buy the biggest box of colors I wanted, flesh, gold and silver. Oh, happy day! Through the years, I have tried many crafts just for my own enjoyment: sewing, pottery, knitting, cooking and gardening, etc. I know a little about a lot of things.

Then I discovered I could express myself by writing. I find writing poems and stories is similar to painting with words. I love stringing a group of descriptive words together that express what I am feeling or seeing at the moment. In many ways it is more satisfying than painting because the gratification is more immediate.

Friends have told me that they enjoy traveling with me because I see so much more than they do when we are looking at the same thing. I create paintings and the written words because it is a way of letting others know what I am seeing and feeling and hopefully touch them in some way. My desire is that my talent brings joy to other people.

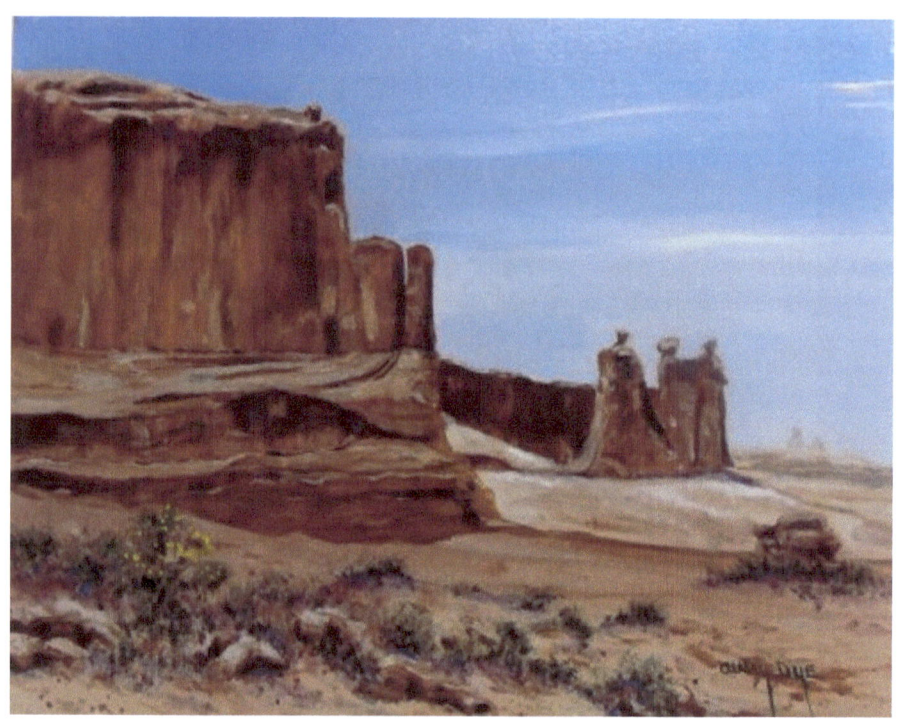

The Pioneers

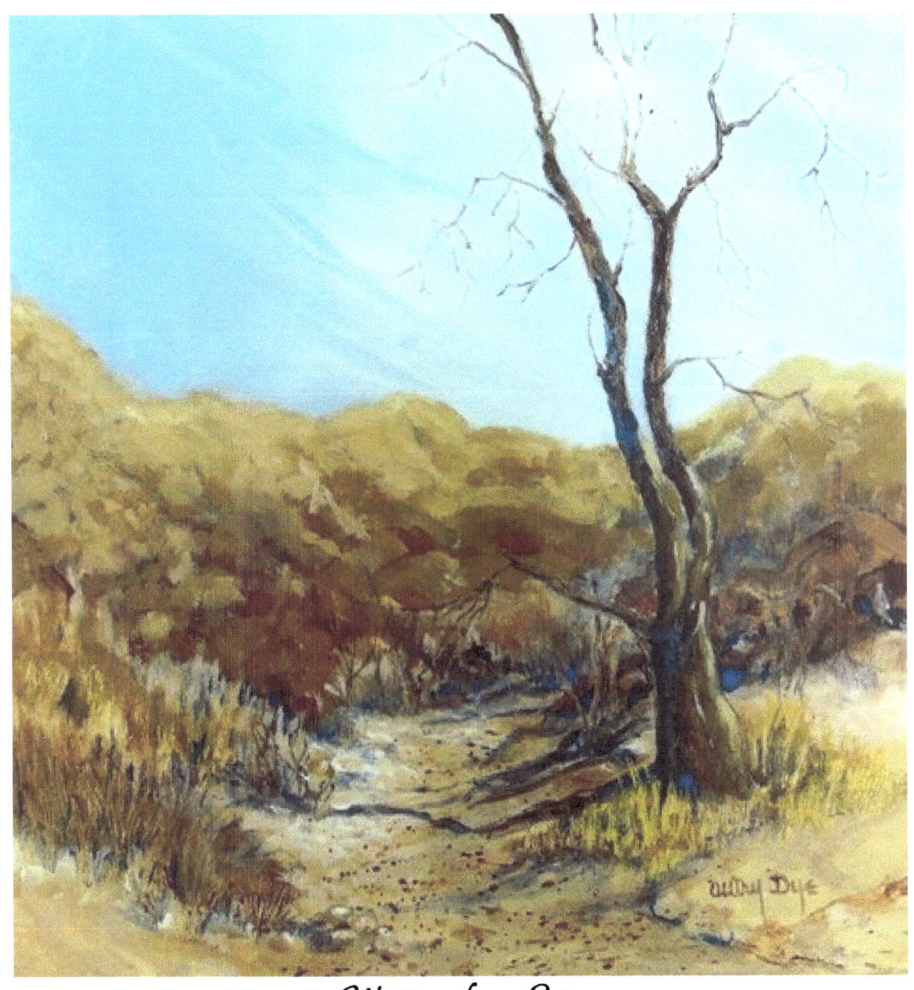

Waiting for Rain

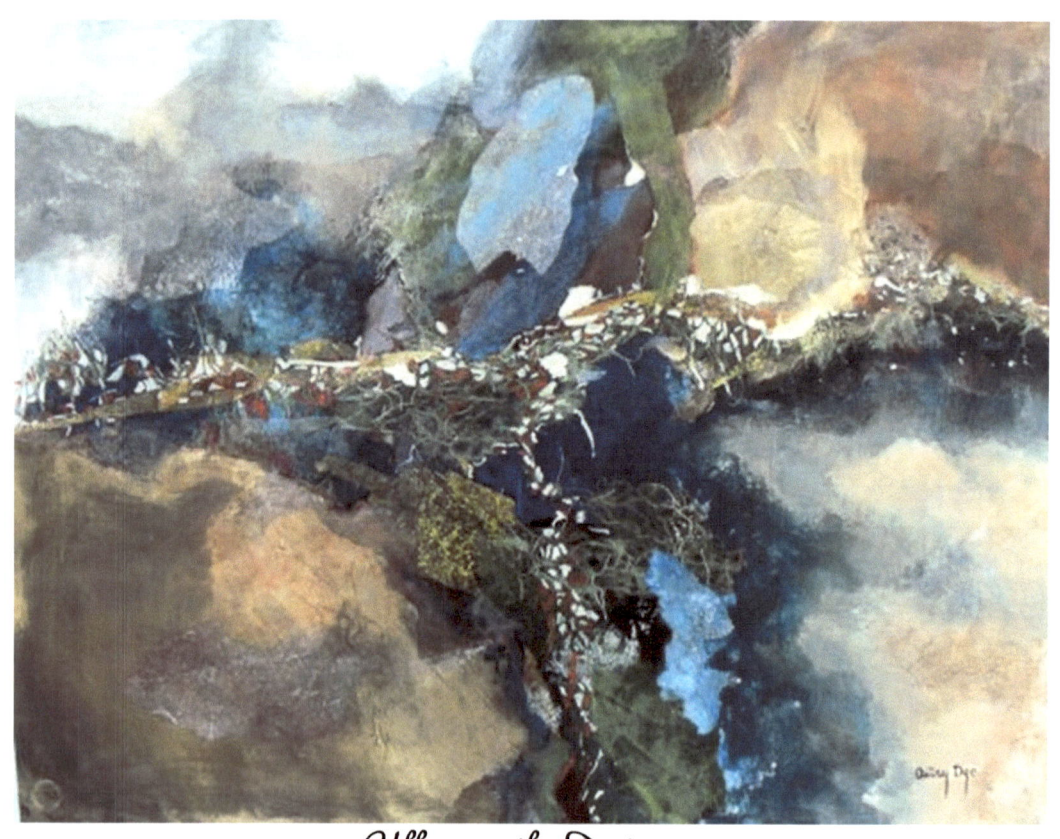

Village in the Distance

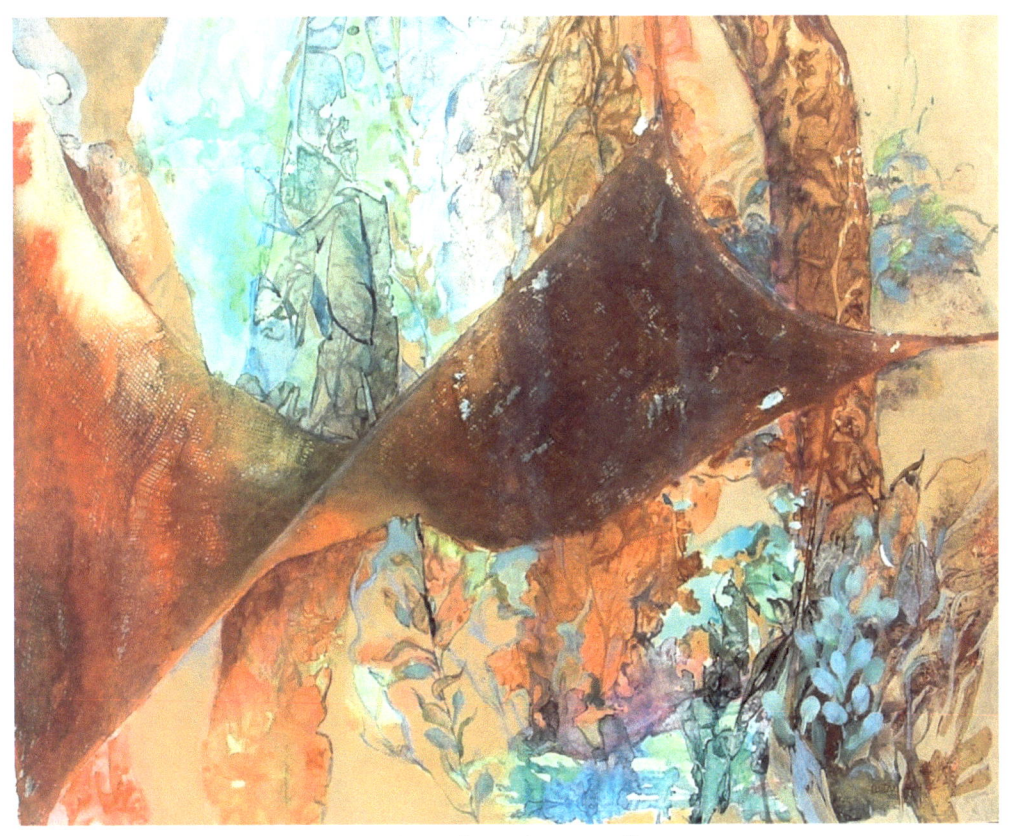

Jungle Hammock

JACQUELINE CAMPBELL
National Member

Art in many ways has always been inseparable from who I am. I believe I've always looked at the world just a bit differently. I think all artists do. I look on my surroundings as not just the world I live in but in colors and possibilities. For example, while painting I can see pink in the hide of an elephant or purple in the trunk of a tree. I find myself breaking down images around me into shapes, angles, analyzing how they "fit" together, sketching them in my head. I know, at least for me, that when I sketch and paint a flower or a leaf, for example, I know that flower or leaf in a way no one else does.

I love these things: being with like-minded, right-brained people, for example, the women in our Pen Women group. I realize I don't have to explain myself or my reasoning, my cluttered art studio, the hundreds of things I collect for "someday." I also love the peace I have when immersed in a project and/or again the art people around me. It's therapy. I also am grateful that I was taught how to paint the Oriental brush way. It's an ancient but still current technique, blending East and West in the strokes. The preparation of the ink and the color chips helps me achieve a centered, meditative, contemplative state. Almost all my brush paintings are on rice paper. The color chips used are from the earth, and then when I'm finished I apply my "chop." Then it's mounted in the same method that's been used for thousands of years. I studied under Newport, RI, artist Bettie Sarantos.

I specialize in watercolor and oriental brush. My first love was and still is sketch. I also have a fondness for photography and capture some ideas for paintings. Some photos, though, have a stand-alone potential. My paintings are in private collections and business establishments in the U.S. and Israel.

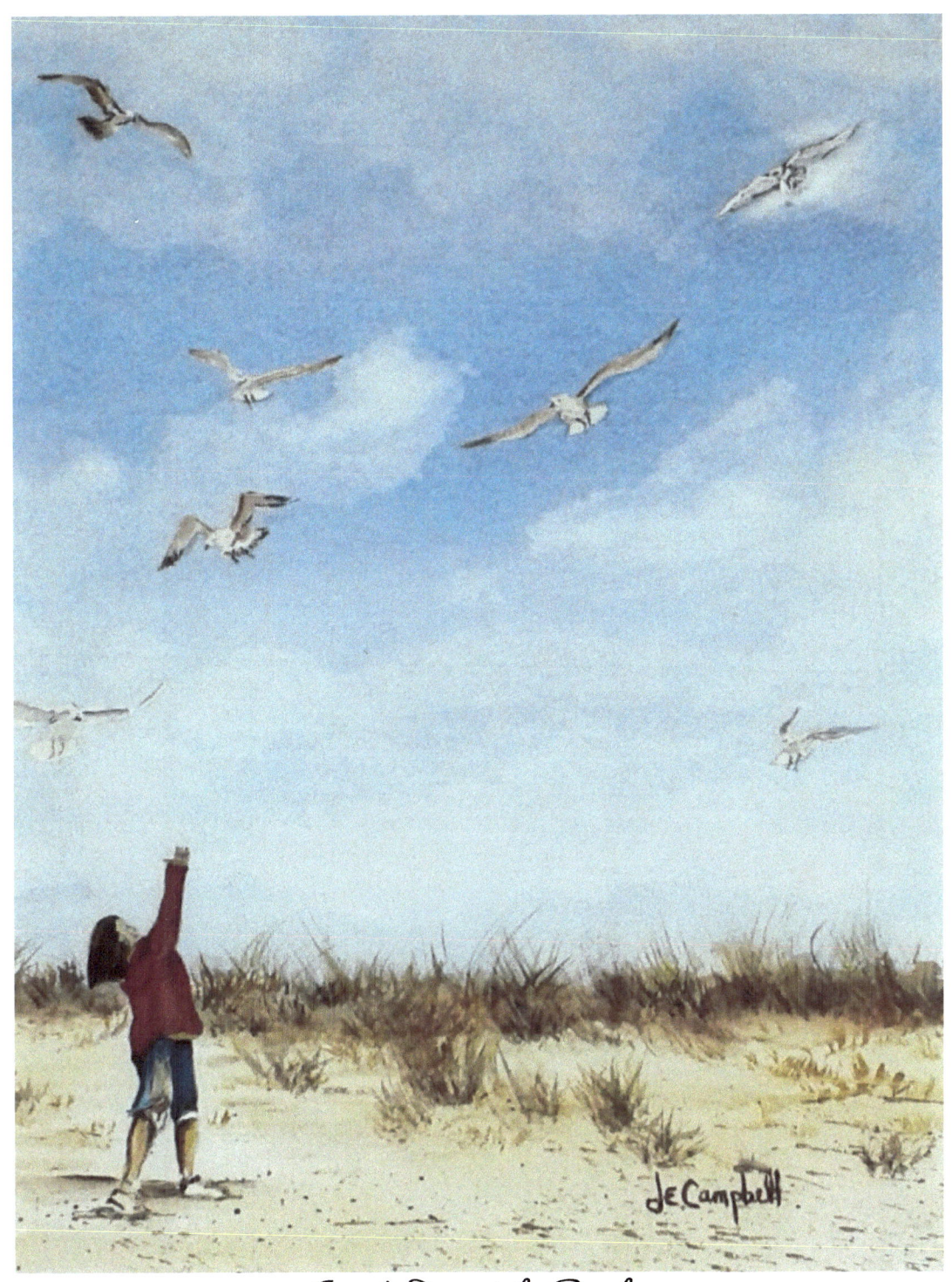

Jessie's Day at the Beach

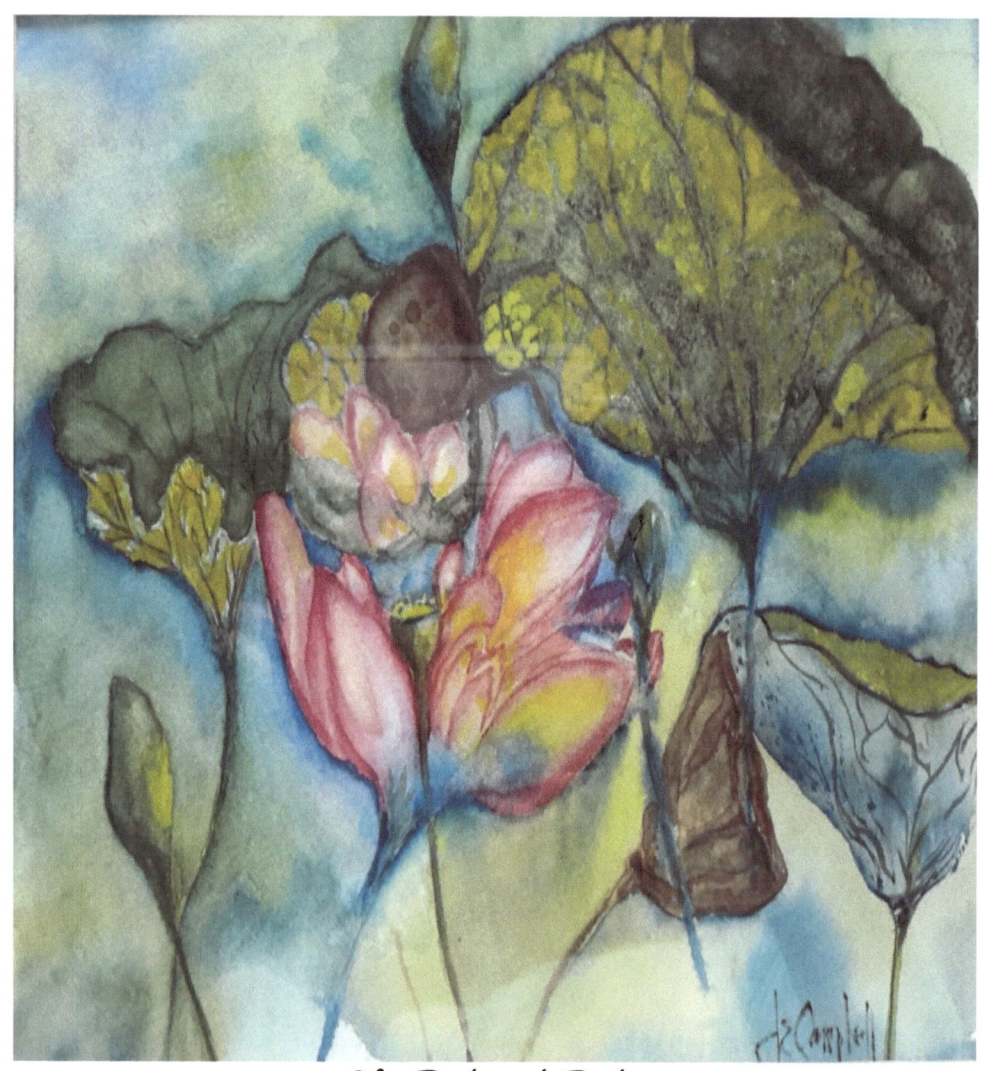

Lily Pads and Pods

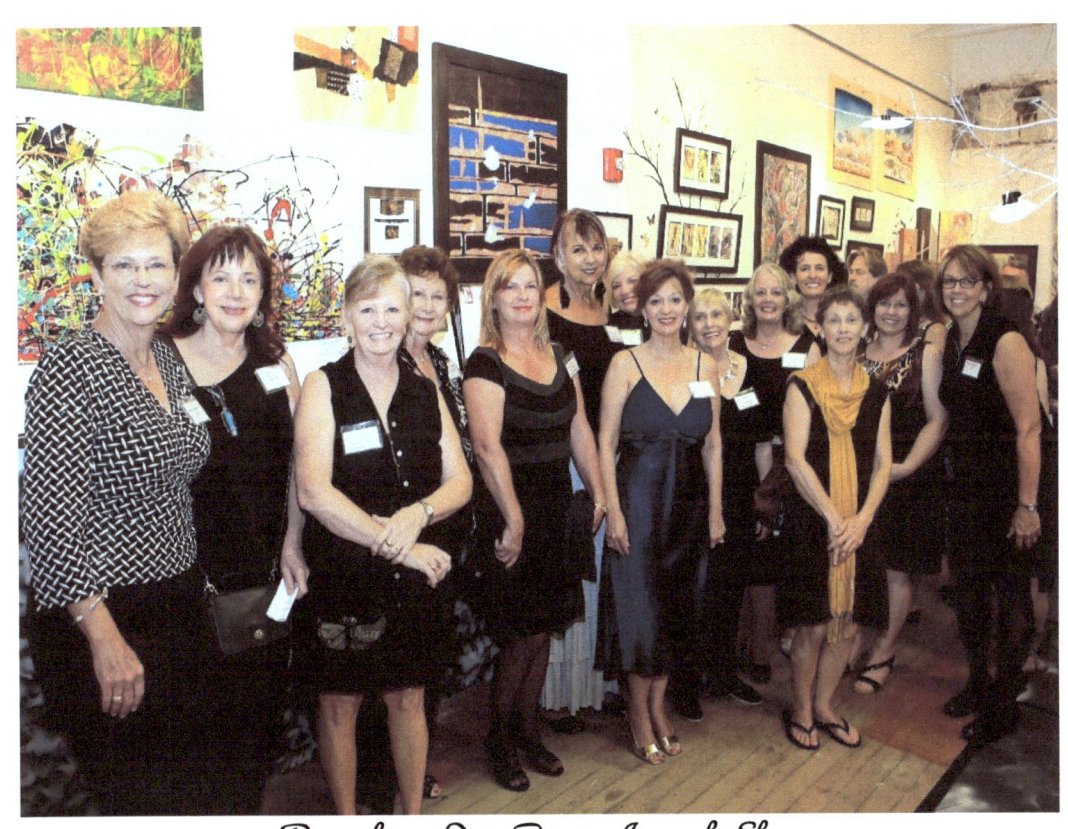

Branching Out, First Annual Show

DONNA FRECKMANN
National Member

Though predominately a mixed media artist, I am also a freelance writer who often uses artists as the subject of my writing, believing the old adage, "It takes one to know one." Best known for my collages, my work has a touch of Oriental flair to it, as I use expensive Oriental papers and Chinese glyphs in my work. Often when I use an Oriental word, I do know the meaning, but I'm just as attracted to the calligraphy of the design that I find intriguing. The Oriental constantly challenges me, as the design associated with this work requires a lot of thought, balance, and harmony.

As the result of some minor surgery in the summer of 2015, I found myself on "house arrest" for over two weeks. Even though I was in a lot of pain for five days, I sat around and did pieces of work for my greeting card line and then went on to do some paintings of wild and funky, bright and happy work. My surgeon says he uninhibited me. I love this new work of geometric shapes and spirals and a few other favorite icons such as fish.

Besides the paintings and cards, I am also a jewelry artist making various beaded items from necklaces and matching earrings to watches. Another favorite in this genre includes pendants. I recently completed a jewelry-making class to augment my other skills with silver and other precious metals.

As a result of two life-threatening illnesses, I developed a workshop for other people and groups that have had difficult challenges in their lives. It incorporates collage making and journal writing—two activities that helped my own recovery. Called Palettes and Pens, the Creative Healers Within, I give the workshops at hospitals and other groups.

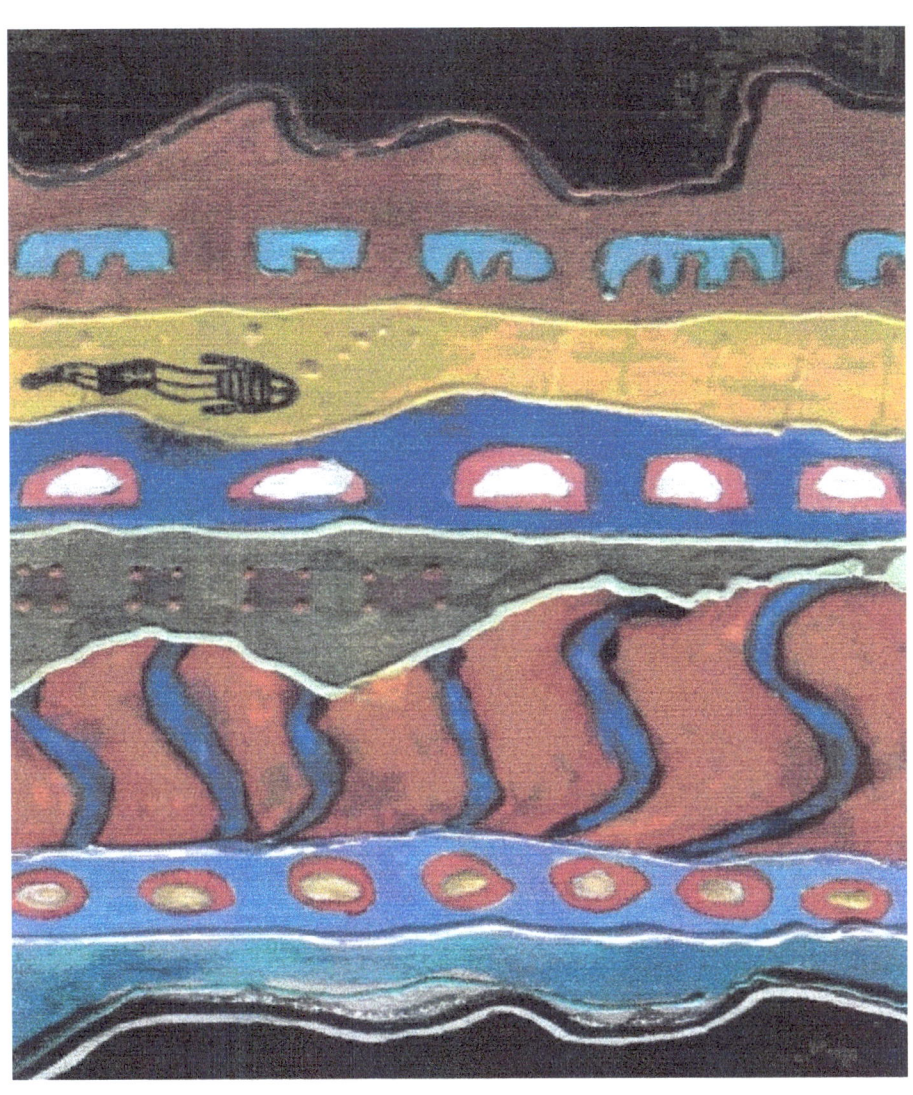

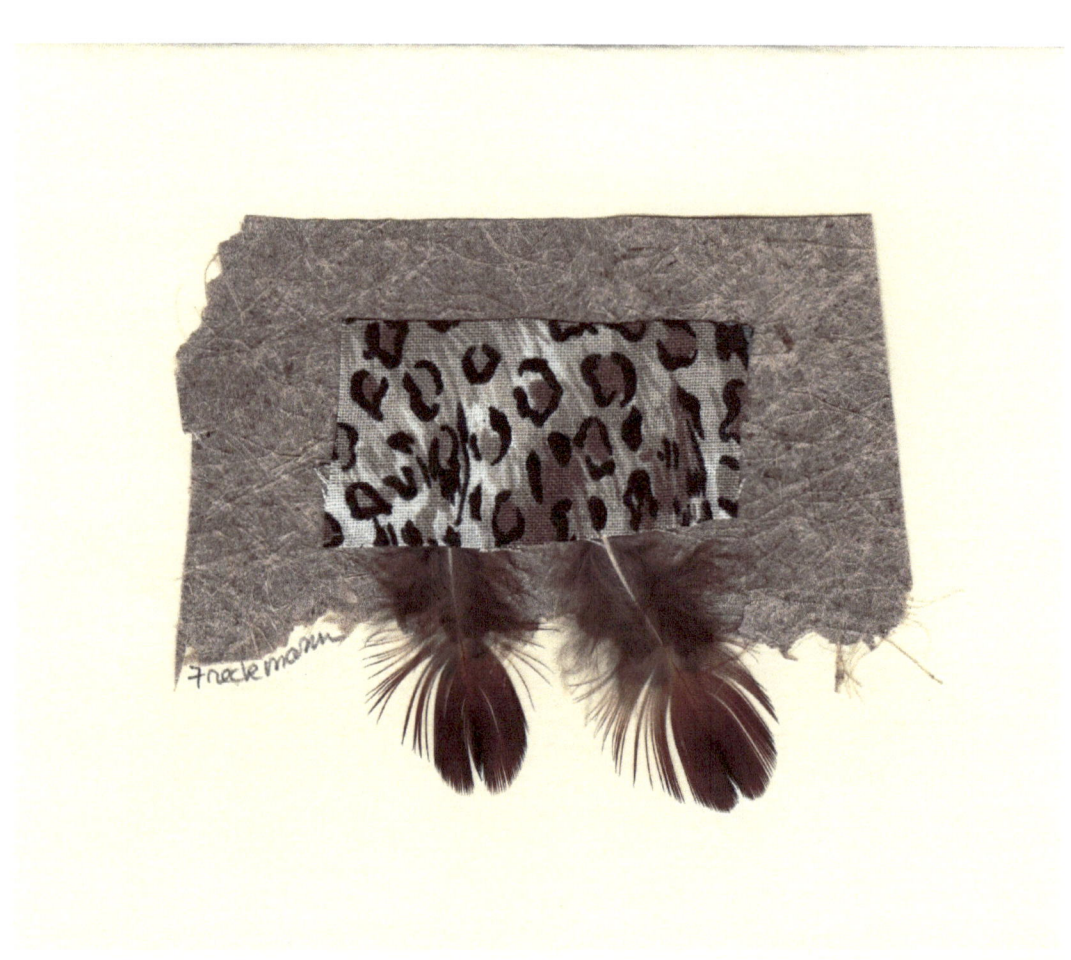

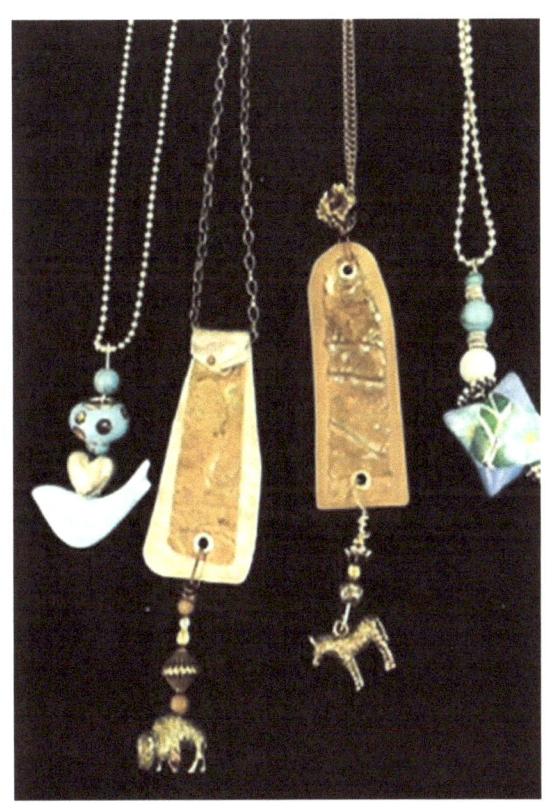

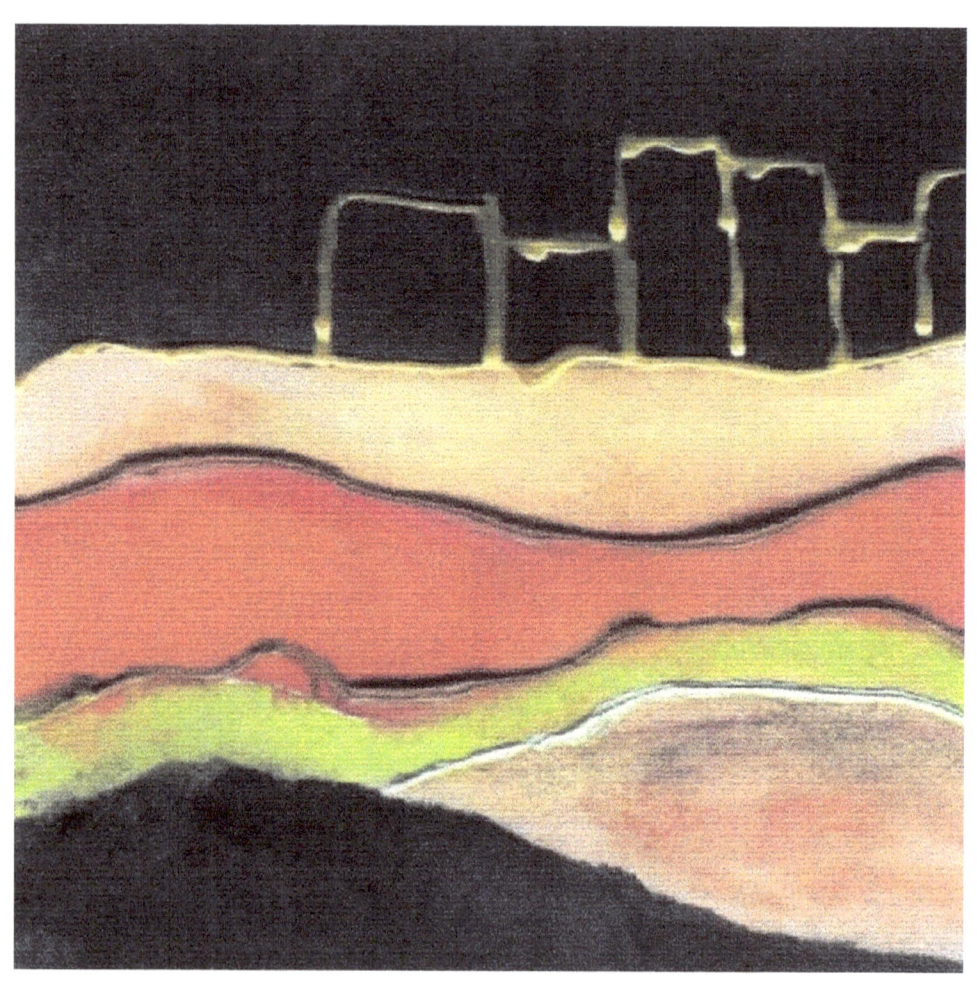

KATHLEEN ELWELL

My joy of painting is seeing the painting as it comes together – rather like a good mystery found in a book.

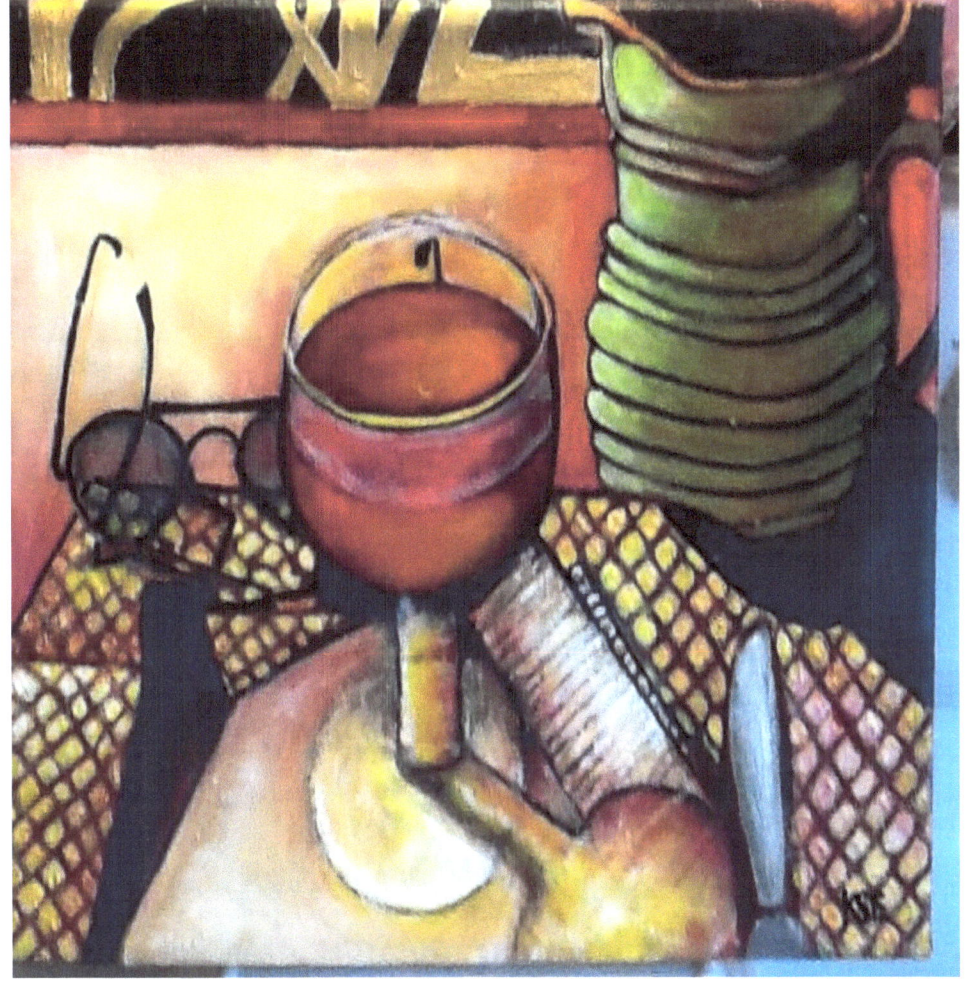

Paris Café

George and Annie

When George died, I cut my hair. I don't know what I was thinking, because I cut my own hair. It looked awful! George had told me my long hair made me beautiful. It's been years since then and my hair has never looked quite as good.

I was the one who discovered George was missing, because I knew his habits; he simply was nowhere to be found. I realized there must be something wrong and I alerted family and friends. Eventually, we found him in the hospital morgue.

George was tall, 6'3" and toothpick thin. His face was weathered, his eyes blue, and his hair brown-blonde. He always wore blue jeans, button-down cotton shirts, and boots.

When I met George, he was trying to adjust to life again. His wife had been dead not quite a year. He said if he could make it through the first Thanksgiving, the first Christmas, the first birthday, etc., he would be Okay. I was responsible for managing the office of two businesses, both owned by the same family. The owner had been George's lifelong friend, and after George's wife died, he spent his empty hours at the office, where he relayed tall tales about his life. He was a natural born storyteller, and we spent endless hours in conversation. I imagine he had always been fun – he was certainly interesting.

Six years earlier, George's wife Annie had had a stroke, and over the ensuing years she developed more complications. Apparently, there were several times the doctors did not expect her to live through the night. She did though despite their diagnosis. I believe she lived to see George yet another day; he lit up her life as she lit up his. She could not breathe on her own, nor could she talk, but they were able to communicate perfectly. He knew the things that counted in her life and it echoed in everything he did. George dedicated his heart, body and soul to Annie. He visited her every day. He only missed three days in the whole six years, and that was when his mother died.

During the many years of his wife's hospitalization, George found himself the only housekeeper at home. As each room filled beyond capacity and habitation, he would retreat to the next room. He was backed between the living room and the bathroom by the time I first met him; everything now took place in these two rooms.

One spring day, I drove George to visit Annie; until then, he had not seen the engraved stone. The sun was shining and there was an easy breeze stirring. It was a beautiful day. We drove about 100 miles. Surrounded by woods stood a white wooden church. On the far left side was a small stand of tombstones. As dried leaves rolled across our path, we walked silently towards the graveyard. I carried flowers for Annie.

We found the double granite marker; there was a vase connecting the two stones. Both sides had been engraved, leaving only George's date of death to be recorded. He remarked on how strange it was to see his own tombstone. I left him there with Annie and went exploring. The next time George returned to the gravesite, he came to stay.

The day he joined Annie, George had driven to the Happy Seven in his copper colored van. The store manager said it was a considerable amount of time before anyone reported him there, still sitting behind the wheel.

He had made it through those dreaded firsts: first Thanksgiving, first Christmas, first birthday, almost completing that first year. He was only days away when he died.

I lost a good friend on that day. Yet George never really leaves me; for as long as I am able to share his stories, all good things about my dear companion will live on.

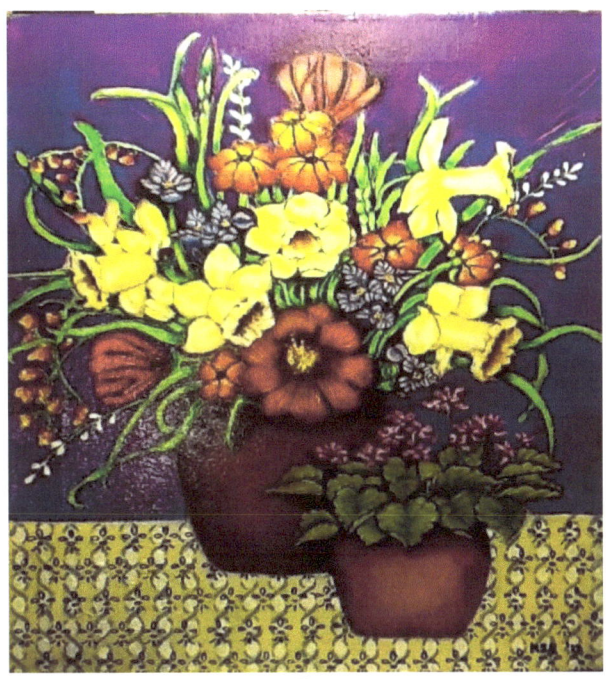

Joy

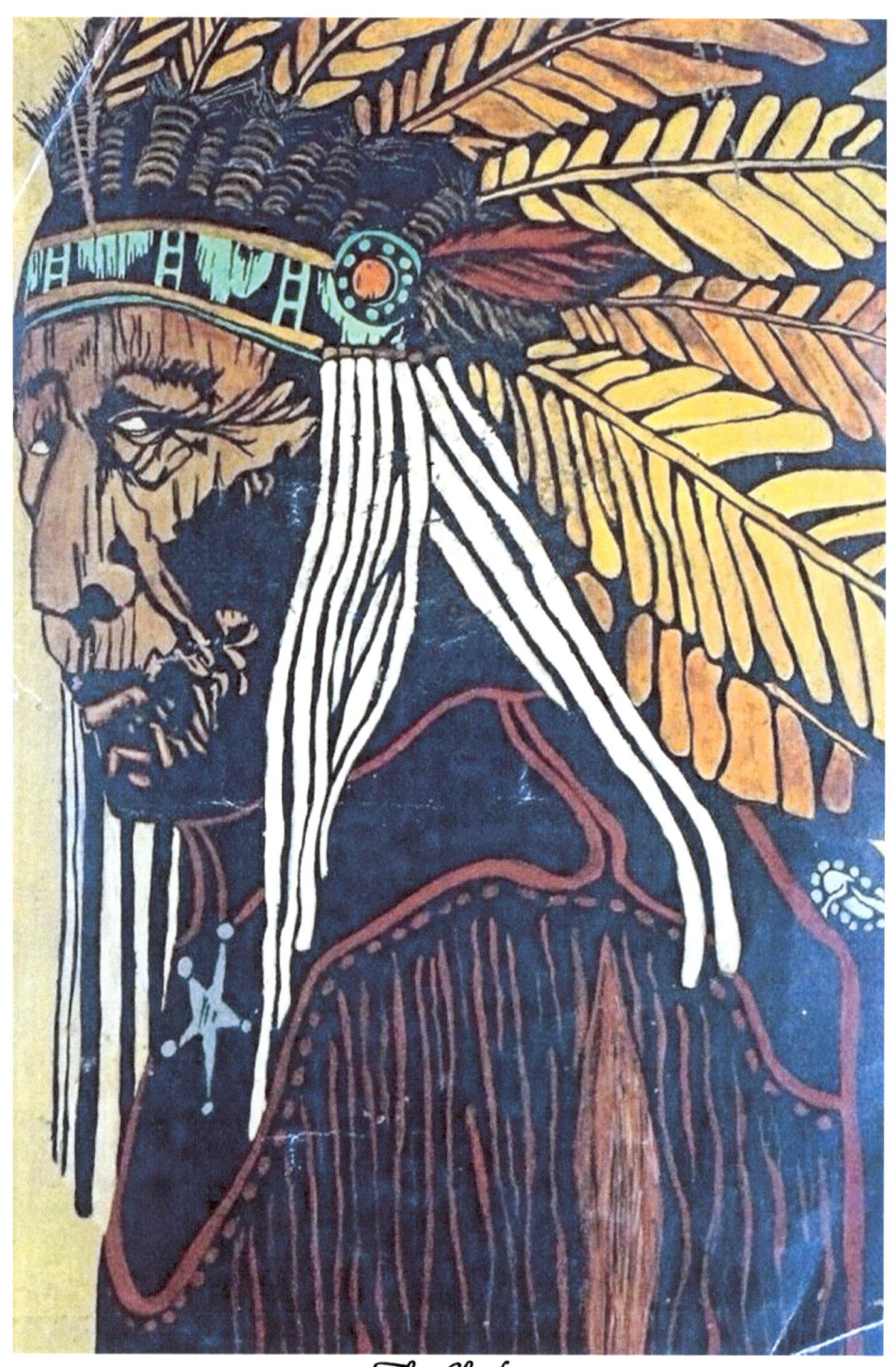

The Chief

BRENDA THORNTON
National Member

My creative interests are in both painting and writing although I've focused more on painting in recent years. Nature is a primary source of inspiration for my paintings, but many man-made objects are sources as well. Often it is not the object itself that is of interest but its texture and the light falling on it. Of course, shape and color are crucial considerations. I like to work a painting to an abstraction even if it starts as a realistic one. It becomes a problem to be solved.

As for writing, I am mainly interested in stories or poems about people and their relationship to each other and to the world. Often snippets of overheard conversation can jump start a poem or a story, or events and people that I have read about in newspapers. In the past, I've tried my hand at short story writing but more recently, I have focused on poetry.

Duo

In the oblivious way of men
He raises an eyebrow,
A friendly sign.
She doesn't smile.
His violin and her cello
Make love
Neither on top nor bottom
But intertwining
As their limbs must
In bed.
"We are husband and wife," he announces
before the next piece.
No surprise there.
The notes themselves copulated.
"Are you the lady who needs a duo?" he'd asked
when the midnight call came
(Though he'd been forewarned).
His wife didn't want to go.
Hard to leave the twins crying,
The laundry undried.
Who knows what might happen?
Her chin rises with the music.
Her tiredness shows.
The long flight from Philly to Atlanta,
Then more driving still.
She is young now.
Her hair falls thickly.
She tucks it away,
A silky drape behind her ear.
Years ahead of dirty clothes,
Of chauffeuring,
Coaxing, cajoling.
She will be a good mother,
There for it all --
Just squeezing in the cello
In her spare time.

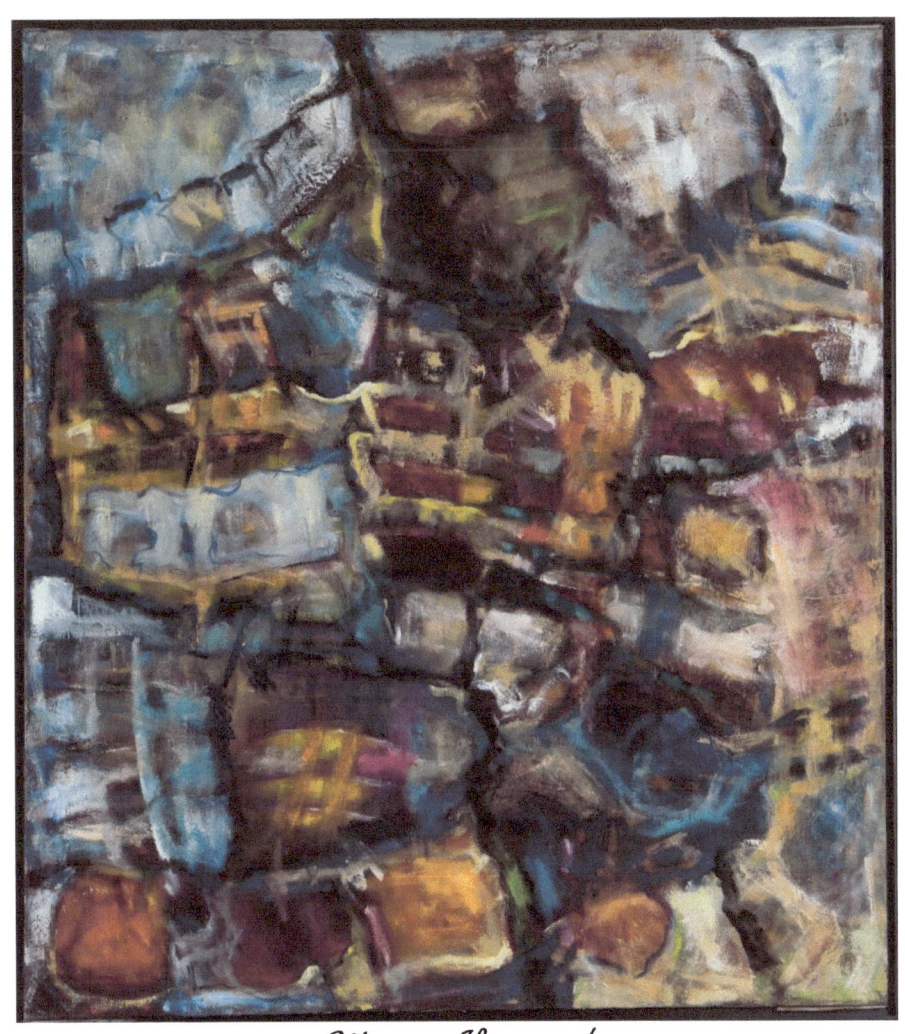

Winter Abstracted

Time Frame

"Do you have a time frame?" she asks at the party.
"My life," I answer.
A puzzled look slides across her face
But she sips her drink.
That's why I didn't go when Harry said,
"You do know what diagonal is, don't you?"
I paused and wondered at the adrenalin rising –
At the anger of old -
Before answering, "I'm not stupid."
"I'm not so sure," he said.

Later in the grocery aisle
My eyes catch in their sockets—
Won't move at will
Or else scat about
With no direction from me.

I try not to think of the man
In gray sweats that bag at the knees,
That sag at the buttocks
As he studies the cost of milk.
For him, perhaps, life is long.
Yet still he eats and drinks.

On the counter are offered
Crumbly almond cookies.
When I bite into one
Oil of almond showers my mouth --
Throws me to a past that never was --
One I only wished for.
And I yearn for it to live

Beyond me in some real way
Outside of me
Even though it never existed --
As false a hope as taste that never fades.

Does the man in the store
Have memory to hold him down?
I dare not think either yes or no
For he has become Harry
Whom before I'd thought cruel
But now, knowing him better
If only in my mind,
I see he's simply resigned.

The Pool

Around your silkiness I swim
Through palest turquoise ruffled water,
Taut and shiny is your skin.
Dart, then glide, past one another
Fleeting touch of hand and limb.

You cup your hands to catch a frog
And thrust him off where he lies flat
On concrete, dead, I think,
His belly soft and white.
We wait and wish it were not so.

A sudden flip onto the grass,
He rests a bit then hops away.

I turn to you who often smoothes
The ragged landscape of my mind,
The you who seems to be so many,
The sum of all the yous I know
That I cannot contain.

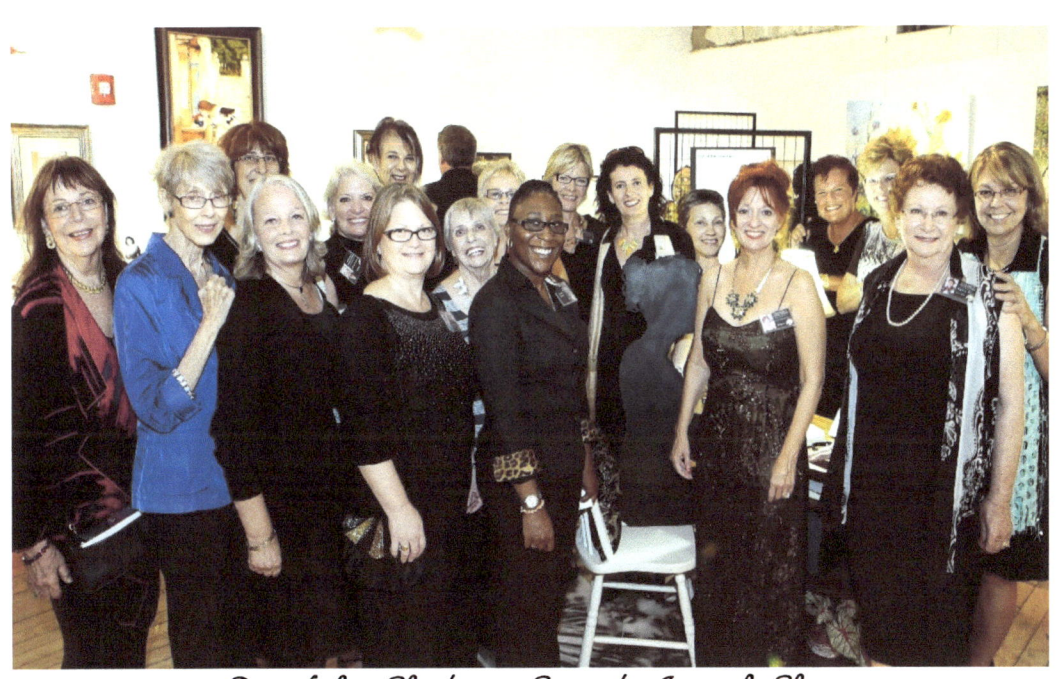

Out of the Shadows, Second Annual Show

PAM WYNN, TREASURER
National Member

I am a mixed media artist working in polymer clay since 1992. Working with polymer clay has allowed me to express my love of abstract art, one of the purest forms of expression. I can communicate feelings and emotions that I cannot express through words. My favorite brand of polymer clay is Premo. I love its quality, strength, and durability, and it comes in an artist array of colors. I prefer to mix my own colors by experimentation. Using a motorized pasta machine, I can knead, blend, and roll out thin sheets of clay that I stack and form into a Mokume' Gane design. My passion is bead making. I create beads for jewelry designers to use in their creations as well as my own jewelry designs.

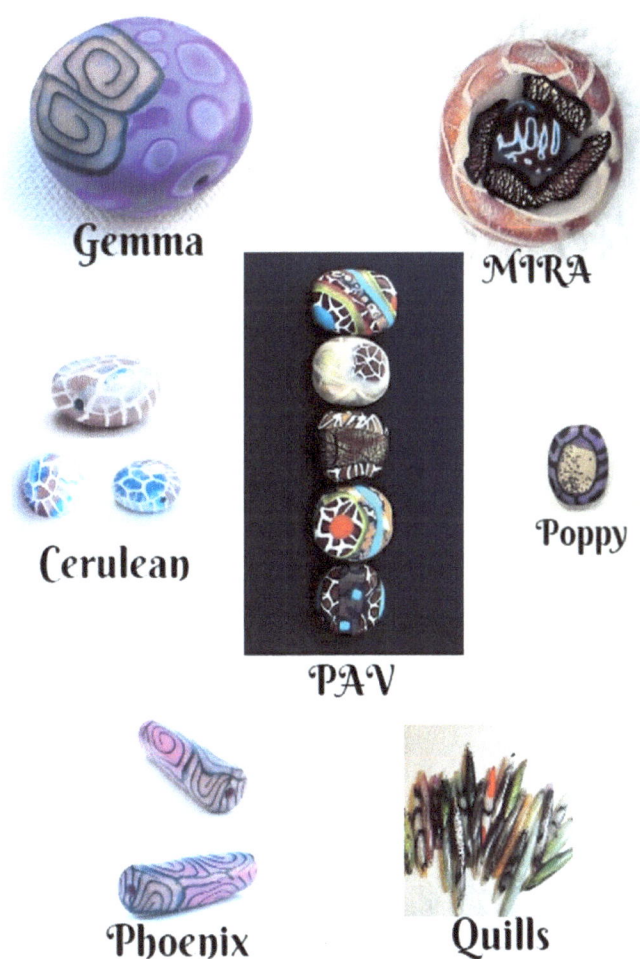

Gemma

MIRA

Cerulean

PAV

Poppy

Phoenix

Quills

Beads by Pam Wynn
Photo Collage by Cassandra Buck

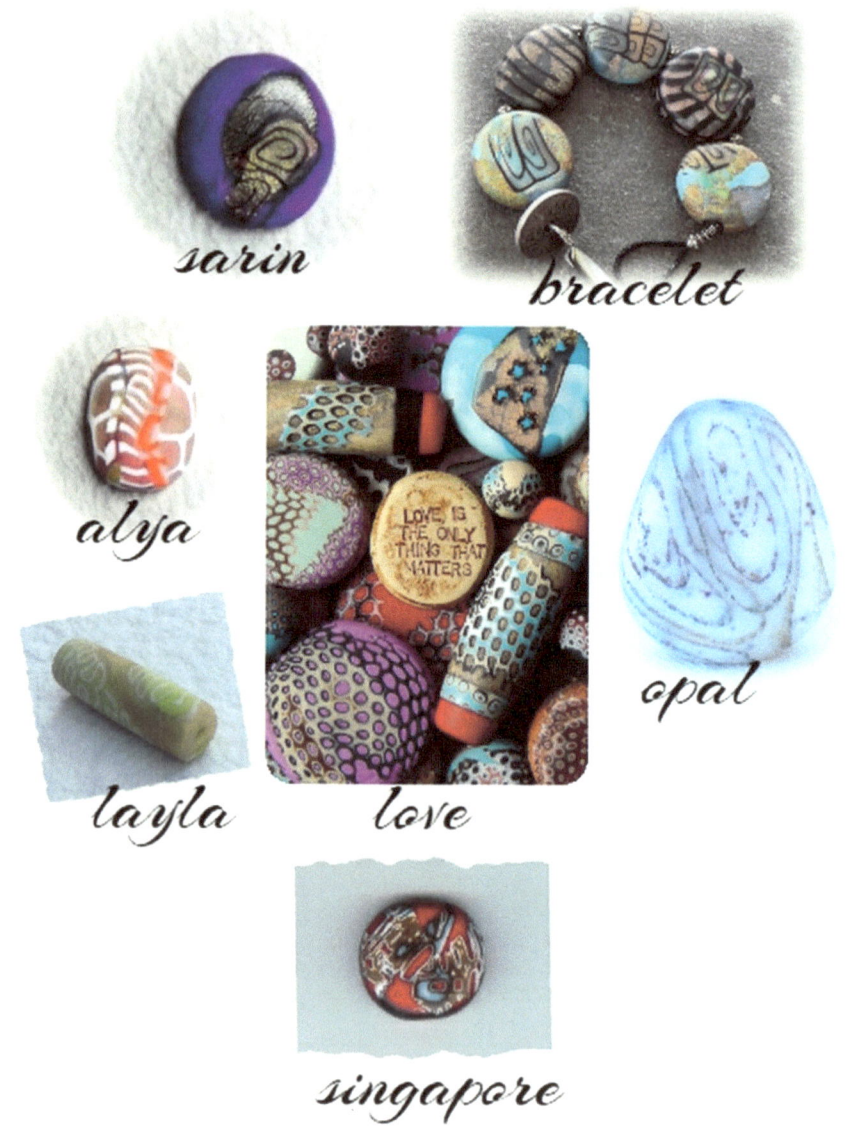

sarin

bracelet

alya

layla

love

opal

singapore

LOVE IS THE ONLY THING THAT MATTERS

Beads by Pam Wynn
Photo Collage by Cassandra Buck

JUDY EGGART

I opened my costume business, Off the Wall Costume Design, on a whim. I had been designing and creating Mardi Gras costumes for several years and felt like it just might be my calling.

I was doing local animal mascot costumes, but I really wanted to reach a national audience, so I boldly signed up for a national trade show in Atlanta for broadcast and marketing executives, and filled up my booth with all kinds of furry creatures. The first genteman who came by said he was with the Boston Celtics and wanted giant heads of all of the starting lineup! I honestly told him I had never sculptured a human likeness before, but he believed in me and wanted to see a Larry Bird head.

I rushed home from the show, sat down with my electric knife, a huge block of foam, and a picture of Larry Bird. I sculpted without stopping. There was foam flying all over like a snowstorm!

Finally I laid my knife down. I was breathless! My kids said, "Gee, Mom, it looks just like him!" As they say, "out of the mouth of babes." The Celtics ordered the whole starting lineup and also insisted I come for the opening of the season party in Boston.

That was just the beginning of my career as a sculptor. And out of that became a professional speaking career that took me to over 50 cities nationwide. I love comedy and making people laugh with a self-deprecating view of my accomplishments.

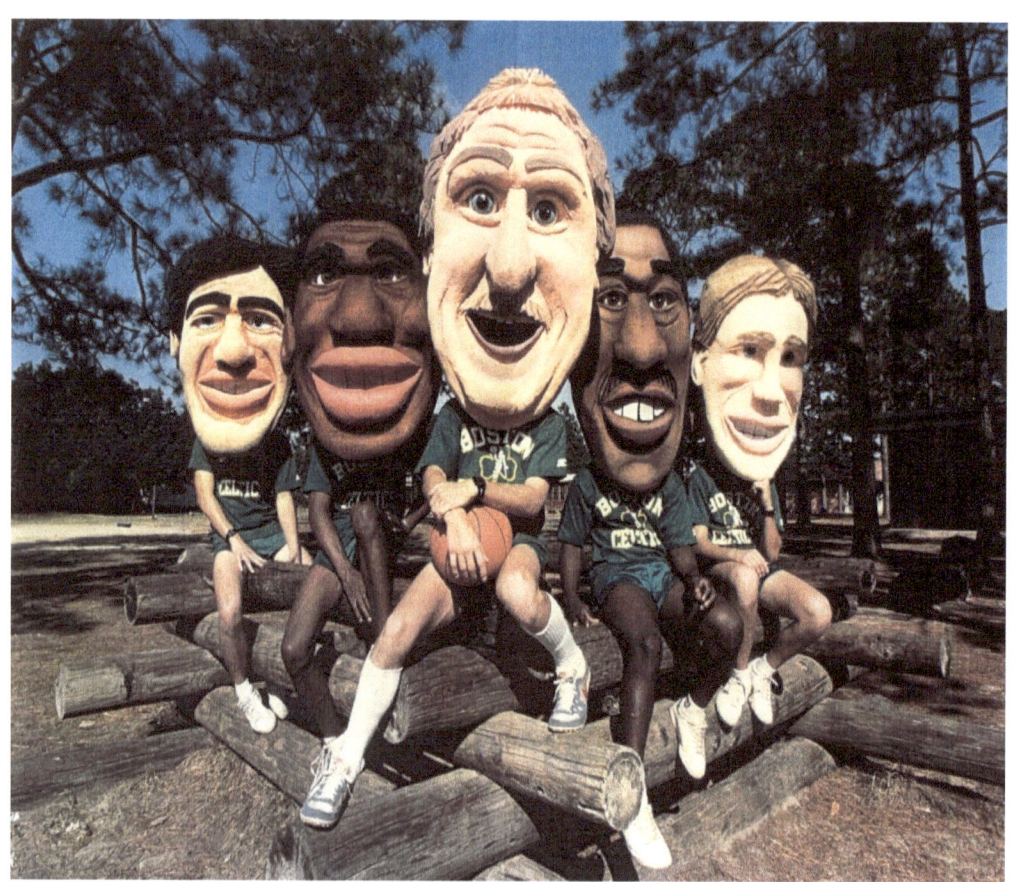

Boston Celtics

The First Thanksgiving

The story of the first Thanksgiving really begins with the grueling voyage of the *Mayflower* to the New World. Conditions aboard ship were dreadful, and seasickness had been rampant. Finally, in the fall of 1692 the colonists reached the coast of America. They arrived too late in the year to plant crops, and they starved through a brutally cold winter. Come springtime, sadly HALF of them had died. Amazingly, the other half all seemed quite plump and happy, with glowing pink cheeks and looking radiant and healthy!

The Indians helped the colonists plant their crops--corn, wheat, pumpkins, pot, and mangoes. And that fall a bountiful harvest it was! Both the Pilgrims and the Indians reaped what they had sown and combined it all for a celebration of Thanksgiving. They had a huge banquet! The Indians had killed many turkeys. (NOTE: The term " turkey" at that time meant any kind of fowl--turkeys, ducks, pheasants, bald eagles, buzzards, and chicken hawks.)

The Pilgrims didn't want to offend their guests for fear of getting scalped; however, when sliced open, the buzzard farted a cloud of steam and was particularly chewy, somewhat like at the Griswolds.

After dinner, the men amused themselves with a cockfight. And one musically inclined Pilgrim got inspired by the sight of the two turkeys in the straw. He set forth some lyrics on a goat's hide using a broad-tip Sharpie.

Meanwhile, the Indians bet two beaver pelts on the red-combed turkey to win. The Pilgrims placed their bet of one pair of Dr. Scholl's gel insoles on the orange-combed turkey. Alas, the Indians cheated by blowing smoke signals from the fire directly into the eyes of the opposing turkey. The poor turkey couldn't see a thing! Luckily a Pilgrim hussy had the heart to dab them with a Kleenex.

Since the fight had to be forfeited, the Indians got to keep not only their two beaver pelts but also the gel insoles. Of course these were of no use to the barefoot Indians until one named "Rides with Chaffed Ass" figured out he could put them under his butt cheeks for a softer, smoother ride on his horse. He was really gellin'! And the song "Turkey in the Straw" was forever etched in the memory of the Pilgrims who didn't freeze to death that winter. And by the time "Chaffed" wore out his insoles, they had built a Walmart on the Plains.

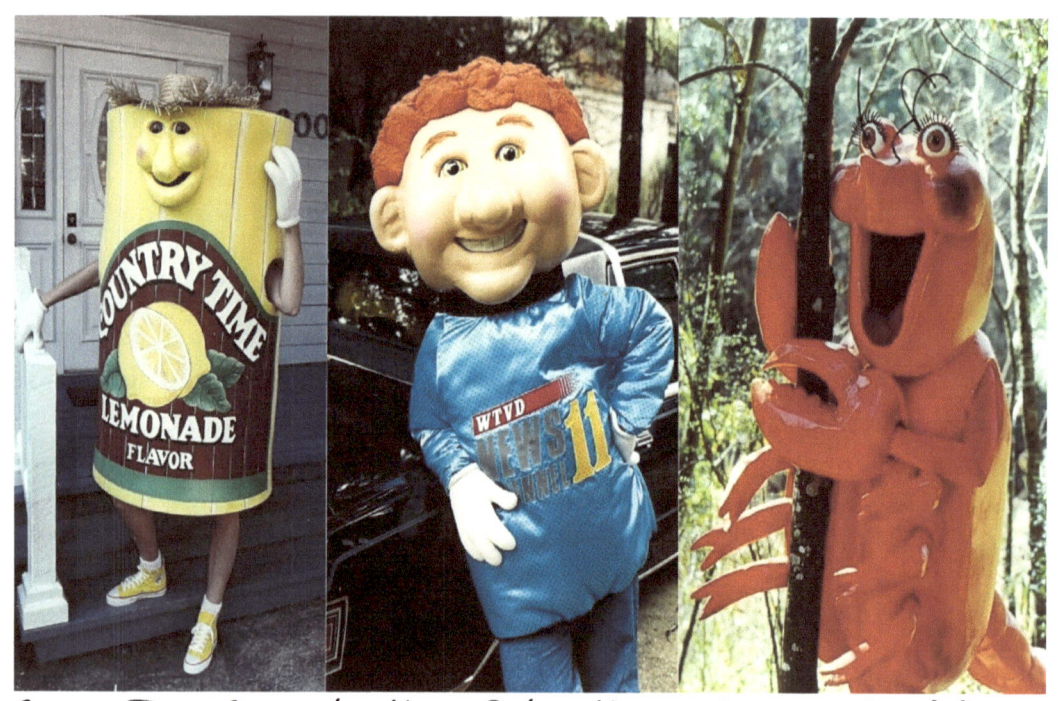

Country Time Lemonade Man, Radio Mascot, Louisiana Crawfish

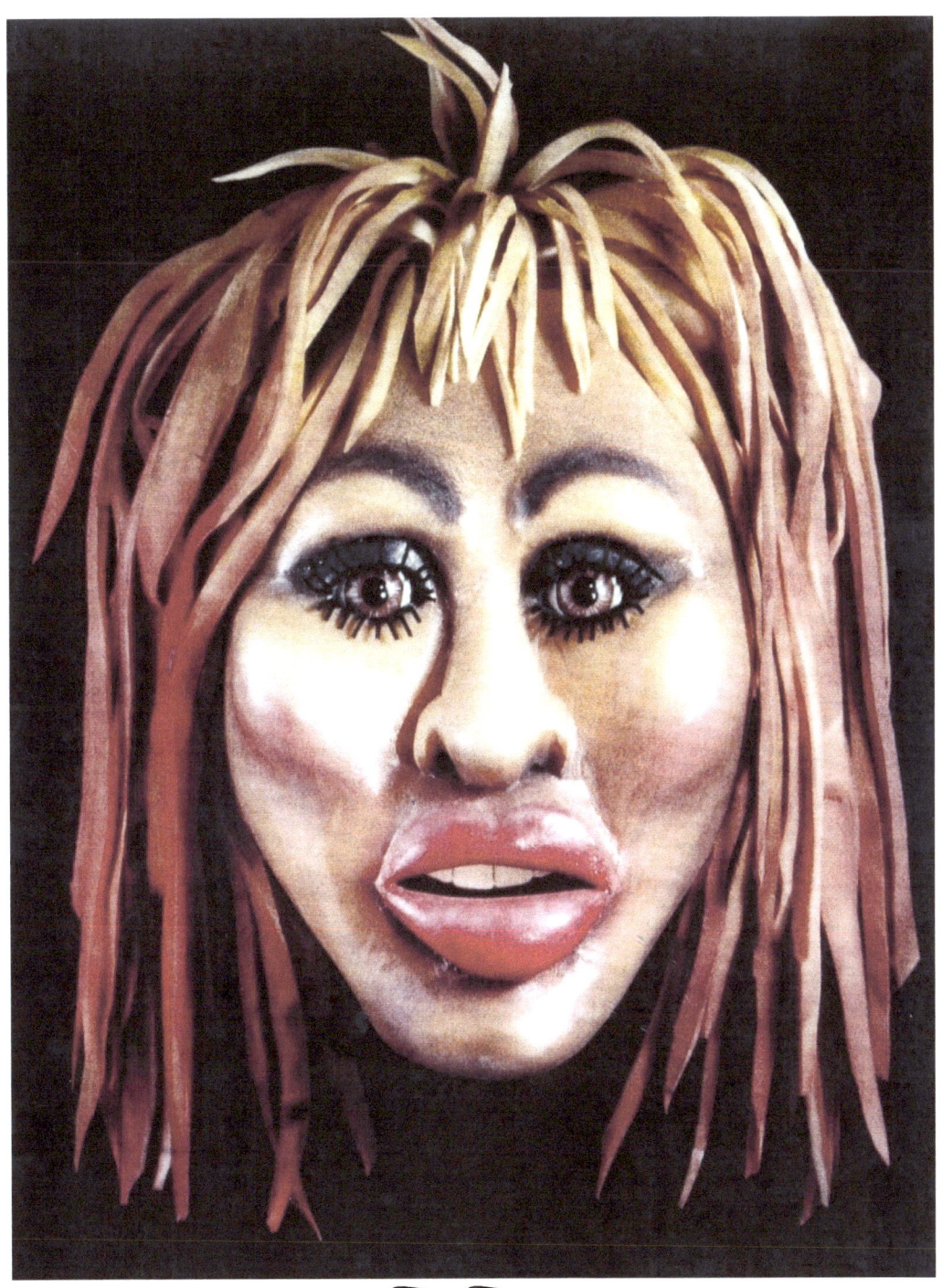

Tina Turner

MELINDA GIRON
National Member

Most of my artistic style has evolved and grown from determined practice, as well as from utilizing a fine art instruction which focused on acrylics, water media, and oils, as well as on sculpting with mixed media.

Working in a non-traditional style using different types of media helps to add variety while creating, and keeps my mind fresh. I use bold colors and varying textures found in nature, and expressively incorporate them into my work, mostly focusing on details. Nature and the feelings of peace, serenity, and wonder are what drive and inspire me to create a piece that intimately conveys these same feelings.

As a young child growing up at the edge of the Australian bushlands, I developed an early fascination for all things natural. In my teens, I became a floral designer that exposed me to a very hands-on and creative work environment, and whose influence is evident in recurring themes in my body of artwork.

Creating an art piece is a way to explore, interpret, and transform nature's elements that passionately move me. I hope the resulting artwork allows the viewer to share my experiences of the beauty in the details of nature, revealing the wonder of God's magnificent gifts.

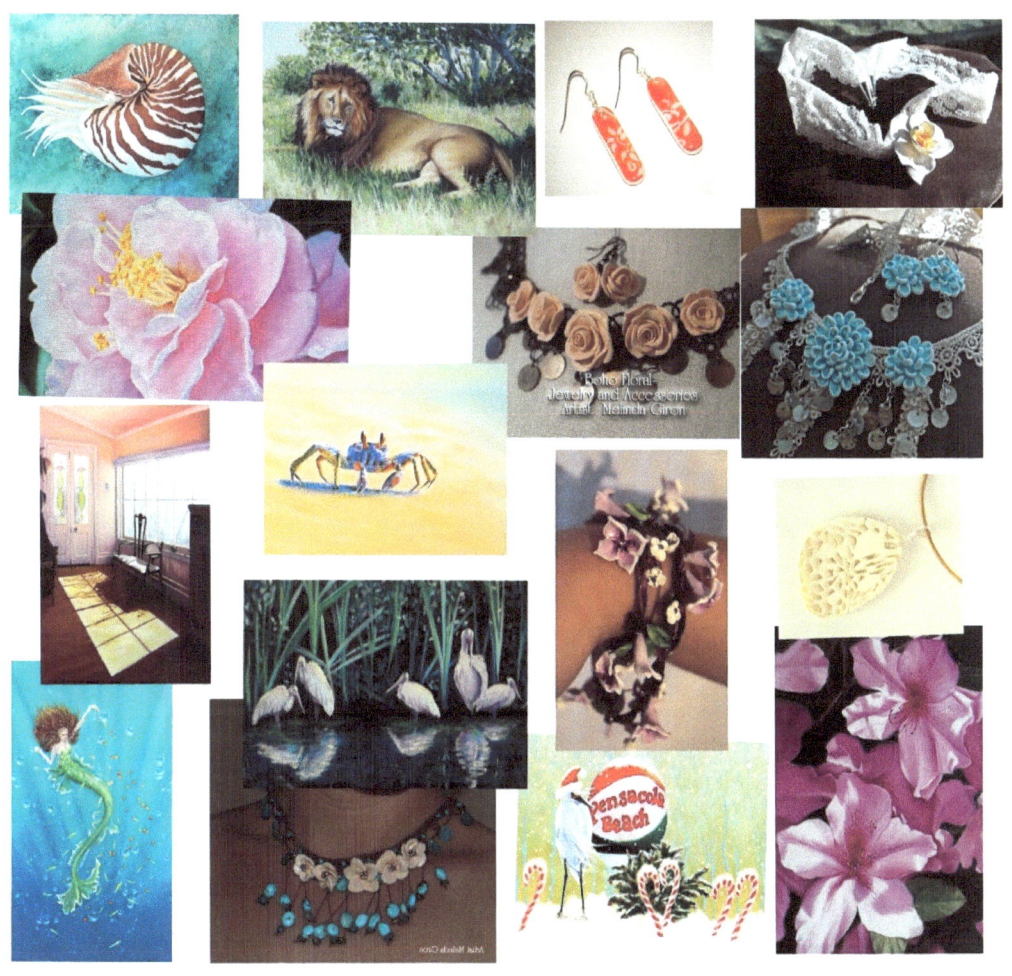

Melinda Giron Art

JACKYE THOMPSON-JENSEN

Art has enlightened my view of the world. Colors, shapes, and shadows are a new wonderful picture of all that I now see. Art has also opened the ideas and artistic thoughts that I feel. The artistic people in my life are a blessing. I hope that I can continue to grow in artistic endeavors for the rest of my journey on this beautiful blue planet.

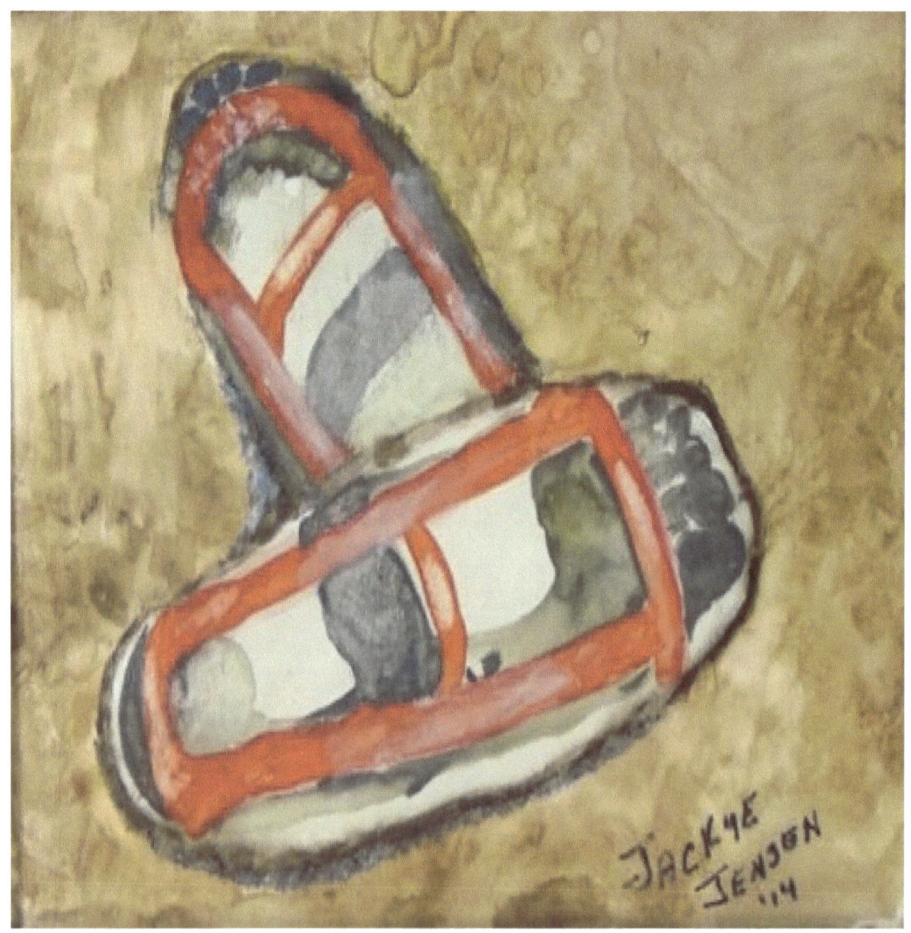

Sandals

Life Journey on Well-Worn Sandals

Infants- Don't need sandals. They have adorable pudgy feet.

Toddlers- Start the beginning of the sandals journey. New adventures, learning, playing, and loving. Walking carefully in these "new sandals."

Childhood- The sandals are now beginning to be a little scuffed, but still in good shape. As a child explores new places, new friends, and the world around.

Puberty- The familiar sandals are part of life and have become a trusted friend.

Late Teens-Sandals are still my friend, leading me softly and well on this world so full of choices.

Twenties- Sandals, you have walked with me through college, new jobs, new loves and lost loves. Sandals, a little more wear with every year.

30-40-50's- Sandals you have guided my walk in happiness, bliss, disappointment and loss.

60's-My dear sandals, a strap is broken, the sole is worn down, time and wear are evident.

70's- Sandals, you are hanging by a thread, a good thread. A thread of good family and wonderful friends. Still learning new experiences for our walk. A love for God and Country.

EDNA PIERSOL-WINDES
National Member

    I am an artist, author, lecturer, consultant, workshop instructor, and juror for national and local exhibits. A National Member of the NLAPW, I served as Vice President of the Pensacola Branch in 1988-89. I have lived in California since 2005, but I was involved in the arts in the Pensacola area for many years. I helped found and design the Destin Fishing Museum, and in 2009 my ink drawing "Destin Concerto" was accepted into the collection of the Mobile Museum of Art in Mobile, AL.

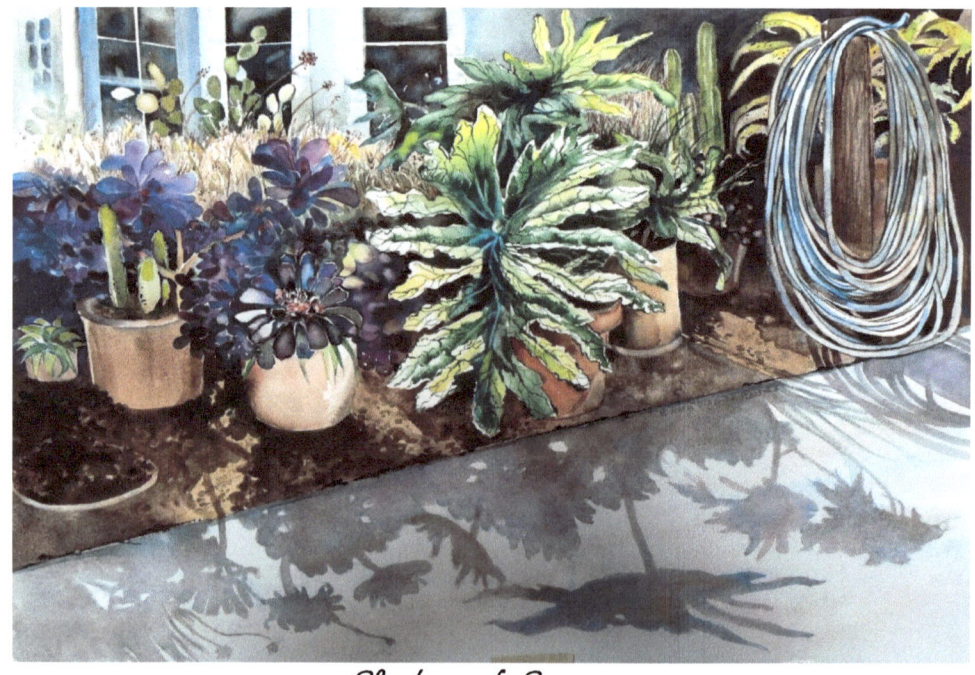

Shadows of Spring

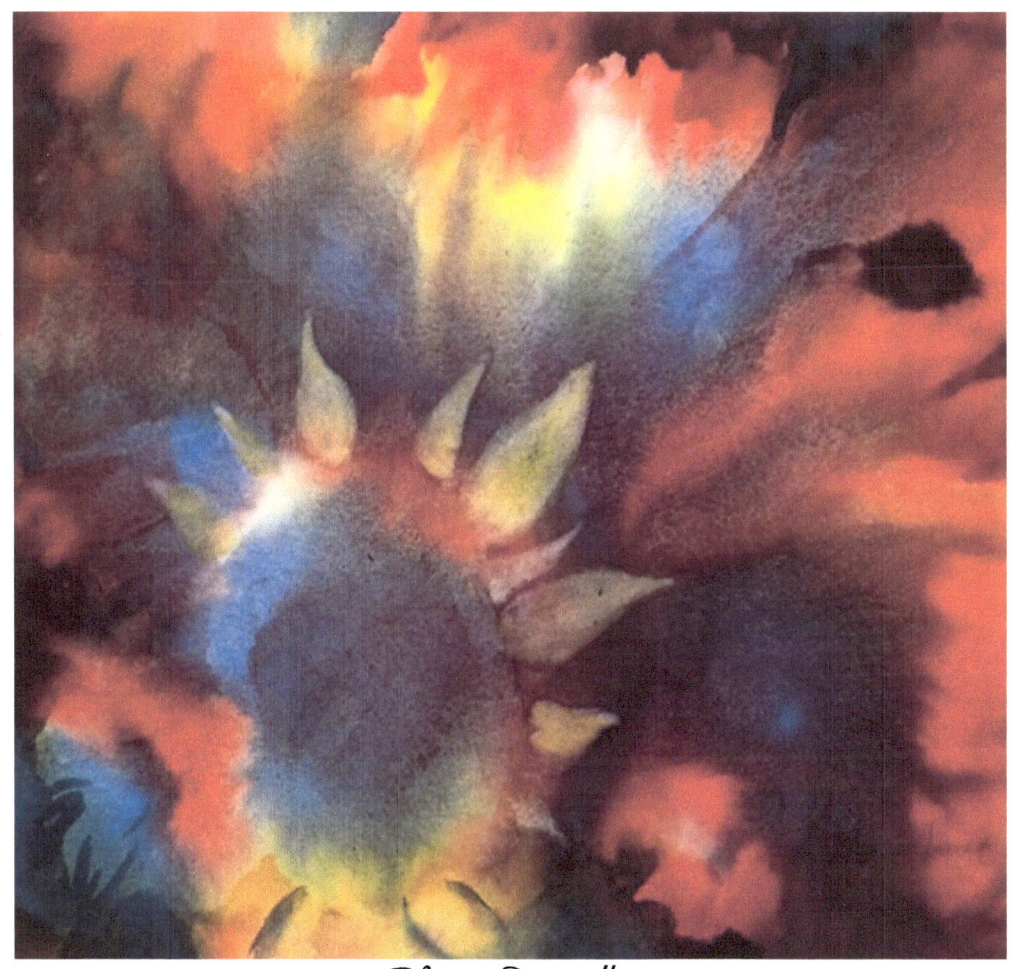

Flower Duet #1

CAROLYN FLEMING
National Member (ret.)

Writing has been a lifelong joy, especially when collaborating with my husband Jack in such endeavors as our books *Perils!* and *Thinking Places,* and the book and lyrics of the musical *Seaplane.* My first novel was *Journey Proud,* set in Georgia in 1933. When I'm working on the plot, I try to remember that life is seldom predictable. Suspense is an inducement to the readers to finish the book.

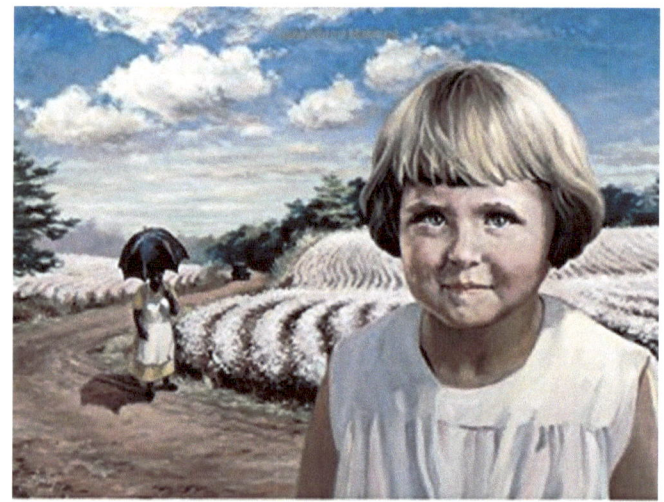

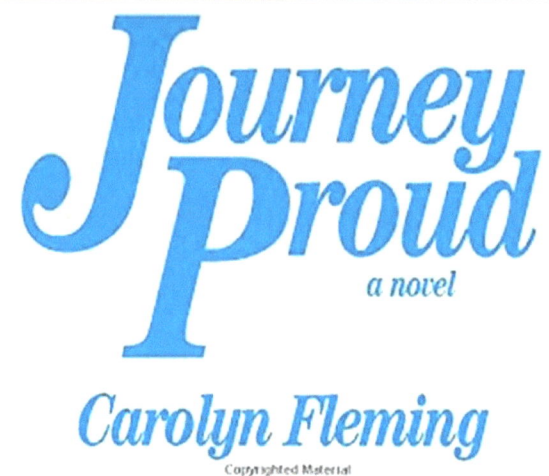

Copyrighted Material

CAROLYN AND JACK FLEMING

THINKING PLACES

WHERE GREAT IDEAS WERE BORN

Grieg...Shaw...Twain...Wordsworth
Austen...Carlyles...Darwin...Dickens
G.Curtiss...Stevenson...Kipling...B.Potter
Yeats...V.Woolf...Thomas...Sackwell-West
Edison...Bell...K.Chopin...B.T.Washington
Carver...Sandberg...W.Rogers...Rawlings
Faulkner...Hemingway...Welty...W.Morris

FOREWORD BY ELLIOT ENGEL

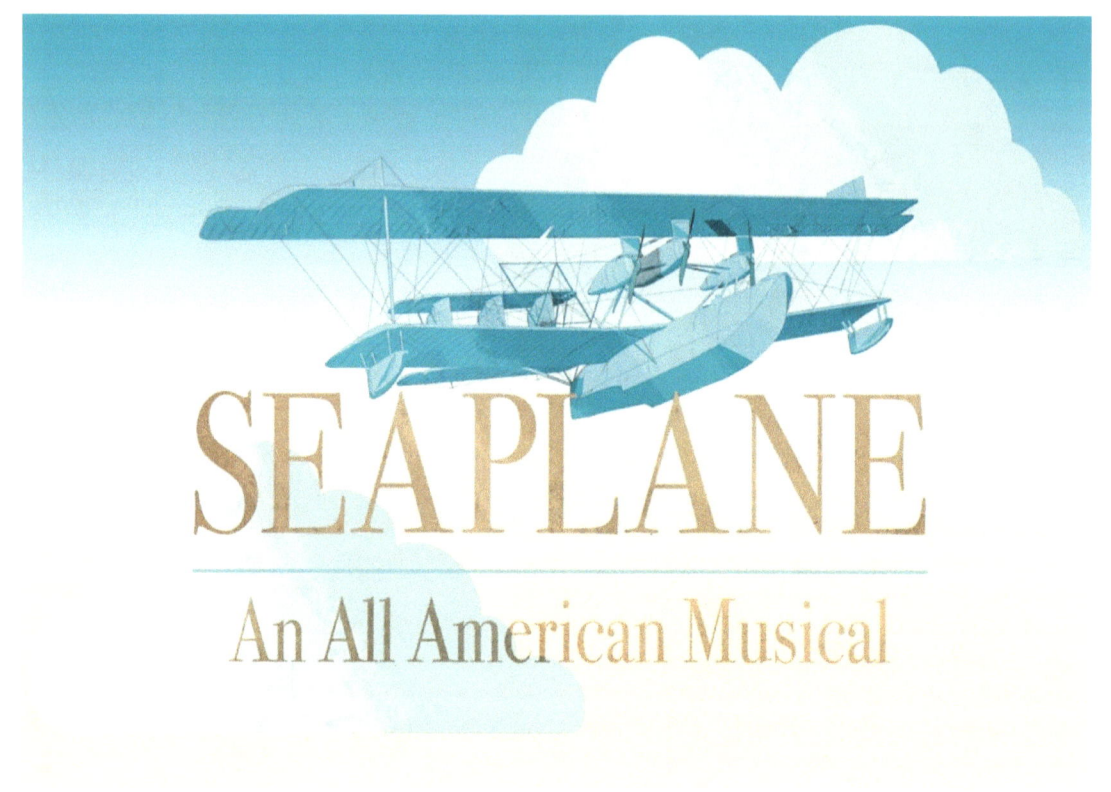

SEAPLANE

An All American Musical

"Art is not what you see, but what you make others see."

Edgar Degas
1834-1917

BIOGRAPHIES AND INDEX

Jane Nowlin (p. 8)

Jane Nowlin was born and raised in Texas. Her family was not the least interested in art. Her love of drawing was an anathema to her parents and others in her family. She didn't like country and western music, and this was even more a sign she was a rebel. She was tutored for a time by a stepfather who was also sort of an odd duck to others in the family because he loved to draw and paint, too. He grudgingly let her use his supplies and studio space but complained that she was too talkative...Imagine that. He shared his knowledge of art with her, and the lessons were Jane's first introduction to concepts and why one needs to study in order to make art well.

Jane left home for the Navy in 1961, the year she graduated from high school. It wasn't until 1966 that Jane realized she was gay and in love with her shipmate Linda. They moved in together in 1967 and remained true to each other for over 48 years until this summer when the Supreme Court decision handed down on June 26th allowed them to marry. They were wed July 12th with many of their friends in attendance. They have lived in New Hampshire, California, Texas, and Florida, and traveled all over the states in their RV. They also visited some of the countries in Europe. They love to go to museums whenever they visit any new state or country. Paris, London, Brussels, Amsterdam, Florence, and several museums in the United States like Boston, San Francisco, Chicago, the Met in NYC, are all on the list of fond memories. Jane loves the MFA in Boston the best because it has the largest collection of Monet paintings outside of Paris. She thinks the Portland Museum in Maine is the most wonderful small museum.

Carol Loethen (p. 12)

Carol Loethen is the owner of Loethen Design. Originally from Louisiana, Carol moved to Florida in 2003 and started designing jewelry. After losing her husband in 2004, faith and a passion for designing jewelry helped her persevere through that dark time. Deciding to pursue a career in art, she returned to school and graduated from Pensacola State College with a degree in graphic design, which has enhanced her skills as a designer and artist. Along with jewelry design and graphic design, photography and mixed media have become passions. If her art and designs put a smile on someone's face, it is one of the biggest compliments she can receive along with knowing she is accomplishing a small part of what God has planned for her.

Loethen Design, 1100 Fort Pickens Road C16, Pensacola Beach, FL 32561, 850-450-1551, LoethenDesign.com, LoethenDesign@gmail.com

Jane G. Lies (p. 16)

Raised in Mobile, Alabama, Jane G. Lies started painting after a move to Plano, Texas, in the late 80's where she exhibited in several juried shows in both McKinney and Plano, Texas.

In Franklin, Tennessee, she joined the JGP artist group who painted at Harlinsdale Farm. While in Franklin, she studied with Jody and Pat Thompson at the SouthGate Studio. Jane was included in the juried exhibit at the Williamson County Fair, and exhibited with the JGP Artists at "Art in the Barn." She was also included in an exhibit at the Jewish Community Center in Franklin.

When she moved to Pensacola, Jane exhibited at Artel, where she won an Honorable Mention award for her collage, "Boats on a Lake." She was also selected in the juried exhibit for the First City Art Show at Quayside Art Gallery.

Anne Baehr (p. 20)

Anne Baehr's love of photography began 35 years ago when she moved back to Pensacola. Capturing nature's beauty, children's portraits, and sports photography are of special interest. She has won local and national awards. Many local organizations benefit from her inspiring videos on their websites. Anne's active membership in the local branch of the National League of American Pen Women has provided experiences in sharing her talents with other women artists and writers, and bringing Arts engagement to her community. She is a member of Blue Morning Gallery and has exhibited in many juried shows displaying her innovative techniques, including Artel Gallery, known for experimental contemporary art, and the First City Show at Quayside Gallery.

Karen Bicknell (p. 25)

Born and raised in Chicago, Karen Bicknell attended Northeastern Illinois University as an Art major, and has continued to paint for the past 30 years. In December 2009 she was honored to have her painting "Vertical Slope" selected and published as the cover of Cross Country Skier magazine. This year one of Karen's paintings has again been selected as cover of the Jan.-Feb. 2016 issue of Cross Country Skier magazine, an acrylic painting titled "The Race." Her other works have been published in Cabin Life and Visitor magazines. Additionally, her work has received awards from Northland Area Art League, Geneva Lake Art Association, and the Cable Hayward Area Arts Council. www.wildpawart.com

Diane Kaye Obe (p. 30)

Diana Kaye Obe was a self-taught artist as a child, later taking numerous art courses in drawing and painting both at Casper College in Wyoming as well as Pensacola State College. She is a member of Blue Morning Gallery, where she participated in three special group shows, and Pensacola's chapter of NLAPW.

Diana has exhibited extensively, including at Xanadu Gallery in Scottsdale, AZ; Soho Gallery, Artel Gallery, and Quayside Gallery in Pensacola; Cedar Chest Gallery in Rawlins, WY; Eastern Shore Library Exhibit in Fairhope, AL; Mary C. O'Keefe Cultural Center for the Arts and Education in Ocean Springs, MS; and Jefferson Davis College in Brewton, AL. Diana also received the Claire Fontaine Memorial Award.

Helen Breton (p. 34)

Helen Breton's career has included graphic design, event production, advertising sales and marketing as well as publishing and editing. Helen is also a Real Estate Broker Associate in the greater Pensacola area.

Maggi Roberts (p. 38)

A former teacher, Maggi Roberts joined the Pensacola Branch of NLAPW in 2014. Through their encouragement and inspiration, she began to show her work. In the 1980's, she owned Chiaroscuro Photography Studio in Atlanta, where she processed and printed strictly in black and white. She shot portraits and ads for newsprint and magazines, her work consisting mostly of corporate photography (portraits) and advertising prints. She spent a lot of time in the dark room producing archival prints. It has been over 30 years since she picked up her camera professionally. With the advent of computers, digital software has replaced the dark room, and large cameras with an array of light boxes are a thing of the past. Maggi now enjoys exploring post-processing techniques.

She shows regularly at Artel Gallery, and had four pieces accepted in juried shows in 2015. Also in 2015 in the 22nd Annual Power of Photography Show at the Pensacola Cultural Center, Maggi received the Mayoral Award for Demonstration of Best Photography and Photographic Techniques from the Florida Panhandle and Southeast Alabama. In February of 2015, she created the Emerald Coast Camera Club to bring photographers together to shoot together, share post-processing techniques and learn from one another.

The club's membership has grown to over 100 members in just eight short months. roberts.maggi@gmail.com/850-748-4886/ Emerald Coast Camera Club, FaceBook Page: **https://www.facebook.com/groups/740989192679807/**

Mara Viksnins   (p. 43)

Mara Viksnins has an Art Degree from the University of West Florida and has studied with many prominent artists nationwide. She belongs to Blue Morning Gallery and Quayside Art Gallery in Pensacola. She has won local, national, and international awards. Mara is also President of the Pensacola Branch of the National League of American Pen Women. She was honored and represented in the NLAPW Biennial Art Show 2012 in Washington, D.C.

Mara also displays her jewelry designs that include wire work using Swarovski crystals, amber and pearls.

Christine Salomé   (p. 48)

Christine Salomé was born in France and is also a Swiss citizen. During the many years working as a French teacher, a "family mother" in two Swiss International Home Schools, and an executive secretary, she used to paint in her spare time.

She has lived in Navarre, FL, for the past 10 years. Now her focus is on developing her art and also on sharing her personal skills as a resource-guide in communication and human relationships.

In June 2014, Christine was honored with a Diploma of Bronze Medal from The French Academic Society Arts-Sciences-Lettres (Paris), and a nomination as United States/Florida Delegate to help American artists' talents be encouraged and recognized in Paris.

In September 2014, she won the Best of Show in Artel Gallery's "Retro" juried exhibition for her photograph "Reflection of Jean Cocteau—L'Inspiration La Femme Peintre, 1961 (Menton, France)" and was honored to have her own solo exhibition "Source de Lumière" in Artel's Award Alcove in May 2015. In October 2014, Christine was honored with the Certificate of International Affiliate Membership in Art from National President Candace Long of the National League of American Pen Women, Washington, D.C.

In February 2015, she received Third Place in the 56th Annual Beaux-Arts exhibition, Arts and Design Society (ADSO), Fort Walton Beach, FL, for her photograph "Above Like Below, Working the Miracle of One (Nice, France)." She received First Place at the 16th Annual Photography & Digital Arts exhibition for "The Big Apple, Light Up Time" (Still Life/Objects category) and Honorable Mention in the "Wee Work" exhibition for her photograph "Sails" in the same gallery.

Christine has also won many awards in fundraising 5K walking races. She is a member of Arts-Sciences-Lettres (Paris), the Arts and Design Society (Fort Walton Beach), Gulf Breeze Arts, the National League of American Pen Women (Washington, D.C.), Pensacola Museum of Art, Artel Gallery (Pensacola), the Navarre running-walking Meetup group, and the Navarre Garden Club.

Ann T. Davis   (p. 53)

Ann T. Davis was born in Pensacola, FL, but has spent most of her life in other locations, most notably Japan, California, and Pennsylvania. Prior to entering the real estate business, Ann's working life was devoted to the field of medicine. Having raised her family and tired of the Northern winters, she returned to Pensacola in 2003 to begin a new chapter in her life. This latest chapter has led to a passion for all things creative in the world of art and encouragement from new friends to continue to seek higher goals.

Nancy Nesvik   (p. 56)

Nancy Nesvik enjoys a variety of painting mediums, as well as photography. She earned her Art/Art Education Degree from Central Methodist College (University) in Missouri, with further coursework in digital graphics at Pensacola State College. She began as a layout artist for Monsanto Company in St. Louis, and after relocating to Pensacola in 2000, she found other outlets including freelance photography, logo design, murals, and her continuing series of Pensacola-themed Christmas cards which she offers in local area stores. Nancy is a National level member of the NLAPW and has been recognized at state and national conferences for her photography.

Kathy Breazeale   (p. 61)

Kathy Breazeale and her husband moved to Florida to open an American art & fine craft gallery in 1991, after she had taught business and social studies in Texas public schools for many years. They enjoyed owning Bayfront Gallery, but after 15 years of the 7-days-a-week pace, the decision was made to retire, travel and explore new interests.

Kathy's interest in the arts as a participant had been in music, and only as an "appreciator" of the visual arts. On a whim, she took up a challenge from an art teacher, to learn to paint. Several years and numerous workshops later, painting acrylic abstracts has become a passion for her.

Kathy recently won several awards at Artel Gallery, including the "Best of Show" award for the "Almost Nothing: Exploring Minimalism." The winner of that award receives a one-person show in The Alcove at Artel Gallery. Her Alcove show "In the Far Away Nearby" was held July/August 2015, and featured abstract landscapes of her New Mexico and West Texas homeland.

After being selected for both The First City and Cinco Banderas shows this year, Kathy continues to examine new techniques using water media.

Linda Devins   (p. 66)

Linda Devins has traveled to most U.S. states following her father and husband from home to home and state to state. A military family always on the move, they spent 3 years in Japan where she was introduced to Japanese art and culture. Linda traveled widely around the countryside enjoying the diverse scenes and the lovely people, and she learned much that isn't available here at home. It still influences her at times when she doesn't recognize it's going to. She worked for Bob Hope as a paid painter and did a painting of the Delores Hope Chapel in Ft. Walton as a commission for her. He liked giving paintings to his guests, and Linda was honored to do them as commissions. She has lived in Mary Esther since 1975 and really enjoys living so close to the Gulf except at hurricane time. There is a strong art community here and she gets great support from her fellow artists. Linda has belonged to Quayside Gallery in Pensacola for the last 25 years and the Arts and Design Society in Ft. Walton Beach about the same length of time. She hopes to continue to create and to learn for many more years.

Karen McAferty Morris   (p. 70)

Karen McAferty Morris has always loved the written word. An educator for 30 years, she taught high school English and Latin in Pensacola, FL. She especially loves poetry, with Millay, Frost, Neruda, and Horace leading the pack of favorites. Now she writes, volunteers, and is working on a line of notecards.

She is a member of the West Florida Literary Federation, Pen Women, and Artel Gallery, and enjoys reading, traveling and hiking. She and her husband, a scientist and artist, live on a little bayou that feeds into Perdido Bay.

Marylin McDonald-Dorsey   (p. 75)

Marylin McDonald-Dorsey has traveled 49 states, memorizing their old trails and forests like a familiar friend's smile. While wandering through life with her beloved husband Ron, she has thrown herself into artistic expression. Marylin has shown her work in many juried shows. She is a member of Artel Gallery, where she won the Edgiest Award for her creation of "Love in the Clouds," which is dedicated to her husband, National League of Pen Women, Tallahassee Artists, and North Palafox Art Gallery. Marylin has had a solo artist exhibit at Raymond James, Tallahassee, has exhibited at Dolce Vita, and is an artist for Fine Art America. Her painting "Celebration at Ellis Island" was featured on the cover of *In Weekly Magazine*, and she is the owner of Glass & Stone Artworks Gallery at the Crowne Plaza Hotel, Pensacola, FL. Her poetry has been published in *New Voices in American Poetry.*

Dona Stenstrom (p. 81)

Dona Stenstrom taught at Pensacola Junior College for many years, and was also active in the Pensacola Museum of Art.

Autry Dye (p. 84)

Autry Dye has lived and worked in Gulf Breeze, FL, since 1980. She has participated in the Creative Capital Workshop, Intensive Studies Seminars in Taos, NM, in 2008/2009, Memphis Art Academy, and has taken courses from Pensacola Junior College and the University of West Florida. Autry has exhibited her work and has won major awards, including Best of Shows, Grumbacher Silver Medallion, The Golden Addy and a Bronze Medal from the Arts, Science and Letters Organization in Paris, France.

Jacqueline Campbell (p. 90)

Although Jacqueline Campbell is mostly self-taught, she attended the University of Rhode Island, and has studied with numerous art instructors as she lived throughout the U.S. A proud National member of NLAPW, Pensacola, FL, branch, she has received various awards and was awarded a bronze medal from Societe'Academique Arts-Sciences-Lettres, Paris, France.

Donna Freckmann (p. 94)

The eternal student, Donna Freckmann has taken numerous art workshops over the years to hone her skills. She holds an undergraduate degree in Journalism from the University of Florida and a masters in Counseling and Human Development from Troy State.

Kathleen Sue Elwell (p. 99)

Kathleen Sue Elwell (KSE) is a native of Florida. She has no formal training yet has won several awards and has been given many one-woman shows. You can find her on Quayside's website or on her Facebook business page, KSE Original Art. Her art hangs in Quayside Art Gallery in Pensacola.

Brenda Thornton   (p. 103)

Brenda Thornton is a graduate of Washburn University and holds a Master's degree in library science from Emporia State University. She is an artist whose paintings have received recognition in national and regional shows. She is interested in both writing and painting although in recent years, she has focused mainly on oil painting.

Pam Wynn   (p. 110)

Pam Wynn has lived in Gulf Breeze, FL, since 1989. In 2001 and 2002 she was selected to represent the state of Florida by designing a Christmas tree ornament for the White House Christmas tree. Pam has sold and exhibited her work in New York as well as through the South and West Coast. Her work has been published in *400 Polymer Clay Designs, Polymer Pizzazz 2, Create Jewelry Pearls, Unexpected Findings: 50 Clever Jewelry Designs Using Everyday Components*, and numerous bead and jewelry magazines.
wynnfour@gmail.com. **http://www.pamwynn.etsy.com**

Judy Eggart   (p. 113)

Judy Eggart has made a name for herself as a sculptor of giant foam heads of well-known figures. In addition to the Celtics, she has captured the likeness of President Bush, Elvis, Einstein, and dozens more. Judy was very honored to receive the Clairol Mentor Award sponsored by Clairol, matching entrepreneurs with corporate magnates.

Judy has appeared on the cover of *USA Today* and *The Daily News*, as well as a feature story on CNN and a rare appearance on *Good Morning, America*. Her first love, however, is writing, which she has done all her life in different genres. Being a humorist at heart, as well as a history buff, she loves writing outrageous historical satires about famous moments in history, such as the Boston Tea Party, the Berlin Wall, the First Thanksgiving, and Washington Crossing the Delaware. She is also working on a book of her exciting career and personal triumphs and tragedies along the way.

Melinda Giron   (p. 118)

Originally from Australia, Melinda Giron lives in Pace, FL, with her husband. She teaches private painting classes on occasion, and accepts commissioned portraits as well as other custom commissioned pieces. Melinda sells her handmade jewelry line through Etsy and also on occasion at Pensacola's Palafox Market on Saturdays. She is a National Member of American Pen Women, Pensacola Chapter.

Email: **Melinda.giron@gmail.com**; Blue Morning Gallery, 1 Palafox Place, Pensacola, FL, Phone: 850-686-5151,

Web : **www.melindagiron.com**; **www.etsy.com/bohofloraljewelry**; **www.bluemorninggallery.com**;

Facebook: **www.facebook.com/PenWomenPensacola**;

Social Media: **www.facebook.com/MelindaGironsArt**

Jackye Thompson-Jensen   (p. 120)

Born in Del Rio, TX, Jackye Thompson-Jensen attended the University of Texas in Austin, first majoring in voice and later pursuing a double major in history and economics. She came to art later on her journey in life. She wanted to learn to paint, but it wasn't until she moved to Gulf Breeze, FL, that she began to take art lessons from Autry Dye. Jackye has exhibited in the American Pen Women shows at Artel Gallery, and has been juried into the Gulf Breeze arts festival. Jackye feels that her journey in the art world is still an ongoing learning time.

Edna Piersol-Windes   (p. 122)

Edna Piersol-Windes has been active in numerous art societies as both a member and leader. She served as President of the Southern Watercolor Society from 1999-2000 and Vice President from 1997-98, an organization of which she was a charter member; she was also its webmaster from 2000-2010. She is currently a member of the Los Gatos Art Association, the Santa Clara Valley Watercolor Society, and the Silicon Valley Open Studios. Edna is the author of *Living by Your Brush Alone* and *Learn to Paint in Five Days.*

Carolyn Fleming (p. 124)

Carolyn Fleming and her husband Jack received the Adelia Rosasco Soule Award for *Seaplane*, a musical about early naval flight. *Seaplane* has been produced three times in Pensacola, and at the Kennedy Center in Washington, D.C., in 1990. Carolyn received the Eric Hoffer Book Award for *Journey Proud*. The Flemings, who jointly received the doctorate of humane letters by the University of West Florida, have made a huge impact on the arts community in Pensacola, with Carolyn also co-founding Evenings in Olde Seville, a popular summer concert series

(

www.ingramcontent.com/pod-product-compliance
Lightning Source LLC
Chambersburg PA
CBHW050718180526
45159CB00003B/1063